812
Con

Connelly, Marc

The green pastures

9/86	DATE DUE		

THE GREEN PASTURES

BY MARC CONNELLY
The Wisdom Tooth

WITH GEORGE S. KAUFMAN
Dulcy
To the Ladies
Merton of the Movies
Beggar on Horseback

THE
GREEN PASTURES

A Fable

SUGGESTED BY ROARK BRADFORD'S SOUTHERN
SKETCHES, "OL' MAN ADAM AN' HIS CHILLUN"

by

MARC CONNELLY

HOLT, RINEHART AND WINSTON
NEW YORK / CHICAGO / SAN FRANCISCO

Thirty-ninth Printing, June, 1971

ISBN: 0–03–028800–2 Cloth
ISBN: 0–03–028805–3 Paper
PRINTED IN THE UNITED STATES OF AMERICA

TO MY MOTHER

CHARACTERS

MR. DESHEE, THE PREACHER

MYRTLE

FIRST BOY

SECOND BOY

FIRST COOK

A VOICE

SECOND COOK

FIRST MAN ANGEL

FIRST MAMMY ANGEL

A STOUT ANGEL

A SLENDER ANGEL

ARCHANGEL

GABRIEL

GOD

CHOIR LEADER

CUSTARD MAKER

ADAM

EVE

CAIN

CAIN'S GIRL

ZEBA

CAIN THE SIXTH

BOY GAMBLER

FIRST GAMBLER

SECOND GAMBLER

VOICE IN SHANTY

NOAH

NOAH'S WIFE

SHEM

FIRST WOMAN

SECOND WOMAN

THIRD WOMAN

FIRST MAN

FLATFOOT

HAM

JAPHETH

FIRST CLEANER

SECOND CLEANER

ABRAHAM

ISAAC

JACOB

MOSES

ZIPPORAH

AARON

A CANDIDATE MAGICIAN

PHARAOH

CHARACTERS

GENERAL

HEAD MAGICIAN

FIRST WIZARD

SECOND WIZARD

JOSHUA

FIRST SCOUT

MASTER OF CEREMONIES

KING OF BABYLON

PROPHET

HIGH PRIEST

CORPORAL

HEZDREL

SECOND OFFICER

SCENES

Part I

Part II

The following is a copy of the program of the first performance of "The Green Pastures," as presented at the Mansfield Theatre, New York City, Wednesday evening, February 26th, 1930:

LAURENCE RIVERS *presents*

THE GREEN PASTURES

A FABLE
by
MARC CONNELLY

Settings by Robert Edmond Jones
Music under the direction of Hall Johnson
Play staged by the Author

*"The Green Pastures" was suggested by Roark Bradford's
Southern Sketches, "Ol' Man Adam an' His Chillun"*

CAST OF CHARACTERS
(*In the order of their appearance*)

MR. DESHEE .... Charles H. Moore
MYRTLE .... Alicia Escamilla
FIRST BOY .... Jazzlips Richardson, Jr.
SECOND BOY .... Howard Washington
THIRD BOY .... Reginald Blythwood
RANDOLPH .... Joe Byrd
A COOK .... Frances Smith
CUSTARD MAKER .... Homer Tutt
FIRST MAMMY ANGEL .... Anna Mae Fritz
A STOUT ANGEL .... Josephine Byrd

CAST OF CHARACTERS

CAST OF CHARACTERS

AARON .... McKinley Reeves
A CANDIDATE MAGICIAN .... Reginald Fenderson
PHARAOH .... George Randel
THE GENERAL .... Walt McClane
FIRST WIZARD .... Emory Richardson
HEAD MAGICIAN .... Arthur Porter
JOSHUA .... Stanleigh Morrell
FIRST SCOUT .... Ivan Sharp
MASTER OF CEREMONIES .... Billy Cumby
KING OF BABYLON .... Jay Mondaaye
PROPHET .... Ivan Sharp
HIGH PRIEST .... Homer Tutt

THE KING'S FAVORITES .... {
Leona Winkler
Florence Lee
Constance Van Dyke
Mary Ella Hart
Inez Persand
}

OFFICER .... Emory Richardson
HEZDREL .... Daniel L. Haynes
ANOTHER OFFICER .... Stanleigh Morrell

THE CHILDREN

Philistine Bumgardner, Margery Bumgardner, Anothony Sylvester, Mary Sylvester, Fredia Longshaw, Wilbur Cohen, Jr., Verdon Perdue, Ruby Davis, Willmay Davis, Margerette Thrower, Viola Lewis

ANGELS AND TOWNSPEOPLE

Amy Escamilla, Elsie Byrd, Benveneta Washington, Thula Ortiz, Ruth Carl, Geneva Blythwood

BABYLONIAN BAND

Carl Shorter, Earl Bowie, Thomas Russell, Richard Henderson

[xiii]

CAST OF CHARACTERS

THE CHOIR

Sopranos—Bertha Wright, Geraldine Gooding, Marie Warren, Mattie Harris, Elsie Thompson, Massie Patterson, Marguerite Avery

Altos—Evelyn Burwell, Ruthena Matson, Leona Avery, Mrs. Willie Mays, Viola Mickens, Charlotte Junius

Tenors—John Warren, Joe Loomis, Walter Hilliard, Harold Foster, Adolph Henderson, William McFarland, McKinley Reeves, Arthur Porter

Baritones—Marc D'Albert, Gerome Addison, Walter Whitfield, D. K. Williams

Bassos—Lester Holland, Cecil McNair, Tom Lee, Walter Meadows, Frank Horace

The Author wishes to thank Alma Lillie Hubbard of New Orleans for assisting in the selection of the spirituals.

AUTHOR'S NOTE

"The Green Pastures" is an attempt to present certain aspects of a living religion in the terms of its believers. The religion is that of thousands of Negroes in the deep South. With terrific spiritual hunger and the greatest humility these untutored black Christians —many of whom cannot even read the book which is the treasure house of their faith—have adapted the contents of the Bible to the consistencies of their everyday lives.

Unburdened by the differences of more educated theologians they accept the Old Testament as a chronicle of wonders which happened to people like themselves in vague but actual places, and of rules of conduct, true acceptance of which will lead them to a tangible, three-dimensional Heaven. In this Heaven, if one has been born in a district where fish frys are popular, the angels do have magnificent fish frys through an eternity somewhat resembling a series of earthly holidays. The Lord Jehovah will be the promised comforter, a just but compassionate patriarch, the summation of all the virtues His follower has observed in the human beings about him. The Lord may look like the Reverend Mr. Dubois as our Sunday School

teacher speculates in the play, or he may resemble another believer's own grandfather. In any event, His
face will be familiar to the one who has come for his
reward.

The author is indebted to Mr. Roark Bradford,
whose retelling of several of the Old Testament stories
in "Ol' Man Adam an' His Chillun" first stimulated
his interest in this point of view.

One need not blame a hazy memory of the Bible for
the failure to recall the characters of Hezdrel, Zeba and
others in the play. They are the author's apocrypha,
but he believes persons much like them have figured
in the meditations of some of the old Negro preachers,
whose simple faith he has tried to translate into a play.

THE GREEN PASTURES

PART ONE

PART ONE

Scene I

A corner in a Negro church.
Ten children and an elderly preacher.
The costumes are those that might be seen in any lower Louisiana town at Sunday-School time. As the curtain rises, Mr. Deshee, *the preacher, is reading from a Bible. The* Children *are listening with varied degrees of interest. Three or four are wide-eyed in their attention. Two or three are obviously puzzled, but interested, and the smallest ones are engaged in more physical concerns. One is playing with a little doll, and another runs his finger on all the angles of his chair.*

DESHEE

"An' Adam lived a hundred and thirty years, an' begat a son in his own likeness, after his image; an' called his name Seth. An' de days of Adam, after he had begotten Seth, were eight hundred years; an' he begat sons an' daughters; an' all de days dat Adam lived were nine hundred an' thirty years; an' he died. An' Seth lived a hundred an' five years an' begat Enos; an' Seth lived after he begat Enos eight hundred an' seven years and begat sons and daughters. An' all de days of Seth were nine hundred and twelve years; an'

[3]

he died." An' it go on like dat till we come to Enoch an' de book say: "An' Enoch lived sixty an' five years and begat Methuselah." Den it say: "An' all de days of Methuselah were nine hund'ed an' sixty an' nine years an' he died." An' dat was de oldest man dat ever was. Dat's why we call ol' Mr. Gurney's mammy ol' Mrs. Methuselah, caize she's so ol'. Den a little later it tell about another member of de fam'ly. His name was Noah. Maybe some of you know about him already. I'm gonter tell you all about him next Sunday. Anyway dat's de meat an' substance of de first five chapters of Genesis. Now, how you think you gonter like de Bible?

MYRTLE

I think it's jest wonderful, Mr. Deshee. I cain't understand any of it.

FIRST BOY

Why did dey live so long, Mr. Deshee?

DESHEE

Why? Caize dat was de way God felt.

SECOND BOY

Dat made Adam a way back.

DESHEE

Yes, he certainly 'way back by de time Noah come along. Want to ask me any mo' questions?

SECOND BOY

What de worl' look like when de Lawd begin, Mr. Deshee?

DESHEE

How yo' mean what it look like?

MYRTLE

Carlisle mean who was in N'Orleans den.

DESHEE

Dey wasn't nobody in N'Orleans on 'count dey wasn't any N'Orleans. Dat's de whole idea I tol' you at de end of de first Chapter. Yo' got to git yo' minds fixed. Dey wasn't any Rampart Street. Dey wasn't any Canal Street. Dey wasn't any Louisiana. Dey wasn't nothin' on de earth at all caize fo' de reason dey wasn't any earth.

MYRTLE

Yes, but what Carlisle wanter know is—

DESHEE

[Interrupting and addressing little boy who has been playing with his chair and paying no attention.] Now Randolph, if you don't listen, how yo' gonter grow up and be a good man? Yo' wanter grow up an' be a transgressor?

[5]

LITTLE BOY

[*Frightened.*] No.

DESHEE

You tell yo' mammy yo' sister got to come wid you next time. She kin git de things done in time to bring you to de school. You content yo'self.

[*The little boy straightens up in his chair.*]

Now, what do Carlisle want to know?

CARLISLE

How he decide he want de worl' to be right yere and how he git de idea he wanted it?

MYRTLE

Caize de Book say, don't it, Mr. Deshee?

DESHEE

De Book say, but at de same time dat's a good question. I remember when I was a little boy de same thing recurred to me. An' ol' Mr. Dubois, he was a wonderful preacher at New Hope Chapel over in East Gretna, he said: "De answer is dat de Book ain't got time to go into all de details." And he was right. You know sometimes I think de Lawd expects us to figure out a few things for ourselves. We know that at one time dey wasn't anything except Heaven, we don't know jest where it was but we know it was dere. Maybe it was everywhere. Den one day de Lawd got the idea he'd like to make some places. He made de sun and de moon, de stars. An' he made de earth.

MYRTLE

Who was aroun' den, nothin' but angels?

DESHEE

I suppose so.

FIRST BOY

What was de angels doin' up dere?

DESHEE

I suppose dey jest flew aroun' and had a good time. Dey wasn't no sin, so dey musta had a good time.

FIRST BOY

Did dey have picnics?

DESHEE

Sho, dey had the nicest kind of picnics. Dey probably had fish frys, wid b'iled custard and ten cent seegars for de adults. God gives us humans lotsa ideas about havin' good times. Maybe dey were things he'd seen de angels do. Yes, sir, I bet dey had a fish fry every week.

[7]

MYRTLE

Did dey have Sunday School, too?

DESHEE

Yes, dey musta had Sunday School for de cherubs.

MYRTLE

What did God look like, Mr. Deshee?

DESHEE

Well, nobody knows exactly what God looked like. But when I was a little boy I used to imagine dat he looked like de Reverend Dubois. He was de finest looking ol' man I ever knew. Yes, I used to bet de Lawd looked exactly like Mr. Dubois in de days when he walked de earth in de shape of a natchel man.

MYRTLE

When was dat, Mr. Deshee?

DESHEE

Why, when he was gettin' things started down heah. When He talked to Adam and Eve and Noah and Moses and all dem. He made mighty men in dem days. But aldo they was awful mighty dey always knew dat He was beyond dem all. Pretty near one o'clock, time fo' you chillun to go home to dinner, but before I let you go I wan' you to go over wid me de main facts of de first lesson. What's de name of de book?

CHILDREN

Genesis.

DESHEE

Dat's right. And what's de other name?

CHILDREN

First Book of Moses.

DESHEE

Dat's right. And dis yere's Chapter One.

[*The lights begin to dim.*] "In de beginnin' God created de heaven an' de earth. An' de earth was widout form an' void. An' de darkness was upon de face of de deep."

SCENE II

In the darkness many voices are heard singing "Rise, Shine, Give God The Glory." They sing it gayly and rapidly. The lights go up as the second verse ends. The chorus is being sung diminuendo by a mixed company of angels. That is they are angels in that they wear brightly colored robes and have wings protruding from their backs. Otherwise they look and act like a company of happy Negroes at a fish fry. The scene itself is a pre-Creation Heaven with compromises. In the distance is an unbroken stretch of blue sky. Companionable varicolored clouds billow down to the floor of the stage and roll overhead to the branches of a live oak tree which is up left. The tree is leafy and dripping with Spanish moss, and with the clouds makes a frame for the scene. In the cool shade of the tree are the usual appurtenances of a fish fry; a large kettle of hot fat set on two small parallel logs, with a fire going underneath, and a large rustic table formed by driving four stakes into the ground and placing planks on top of the small connecting boards. On the table are piles of biscuits and corn bread and the cooked fish in dish pans. There are one or two fairly large cedar or crock "churns" containing boiled custard, which looks like milk. There is a gourd dipper beside the churns and several glasses and cups of various sizes and shapes from which the custard is drunk.

The principal singers are marching two by two in a small area at the R. *of the stage. Two* MAMMY ANGELS *are attending to the frying beside the kettle. Behind the table a* MAN ANGEL *is skinning fish and passing them to the cooks. Another is ladling out the custard. A* MAMMY ANGEL *is putting fish on bread for a brood of cherubs, and during the first scene they seat themselves on a grassy bank upstage. Another* MAMMY ANGEL *is clapping her hands disapprovingly and beckoning a laughing* BOY CHERUB *down from a cloud a little out of her reach. Another* MAMMY ANGEL *is solicitously slapping the back of a girl cherub who has a large fish sandwich in her hand and a bone in her throat. There is much movement about the table, and during the first few minutes several individuals go up to the table to help themselves to the food and drink. Many of the women angels wear hats and a few of the men are smoking cigars. A large boxful is on the table. There is much laughter and chatter as the music softens, but continues, during the early part of the action. The following short scenes are played almost simultaneously.*

FIRST COOK [*At Kettle*]

[*Calling off.*] Hurry up, Cajey. Dis yere fat's cryin' fo' mo' feesh.

A VOICE

[*Off stage.*] We comin', fas' we kin. Dey got to be ketched, ain't dey? We cain't say. "C'm'on little fish. C'm'on an' git fried," kin we?

SECOND COOK [*At Table*]

De trouble is de mens is all worm fishin'.

FIRST MAN ANGEL [*At Table*]

Whut dif'runce do it make? Yo' all de time got to make out like somebody's doin' somethin' de wrong way.

[11]

SECOND COOK [*Near Table*]

I s'pose you got de per'fec' way fo' makin' bait.

FIRST MAN ANGEL

I ain't sayin' dat. I is sayin' whut's wrong wid worm fishin'.

SECOND COOK

Whut's wrong wid worm fishin'? Ever'thing, dat's all. Dey's only one good way fo' catfishin', an' dat's minny fishin'. Anybody know dat.

FIRST MAN ANGEL

Well, it jest so happen dat minny fishin' is de doggondest fool way of fishin' dey is. You kin try minny fishin' to de cows come home an' all you catch'll be de backache. De trouble wid you, sister, is you jest got minny fishin' on de brain.

SECOND COOK

Go right on, loud mouf. You tell me de news. My, my! You jest de wisest person in de worl'. First you, den de Lawd God.

FIRST MAN ANGEL

[*To the custard ladler.*] You cain't tell dem nothin'. [*Walks away to the custard churn.*] Does you try to 'splain some simple fac' dey git man-deaf.

FIRST MAMMY ANGEL

[*To* CHERUB *on the cloud.*] Now, you heerd me. [*The* CHERUB *assumes several mocking poses, as she speaks.*] You fly down yere. You wanter be put down in de sin book? [*She goes to the table, gets a drink for herself and points out the cherub to one of the men behind the table.*] Dat baby must got imp blood in him he so vexin'. [*She returns to her position under the cloud.*] You want me to fly up dere an' slap you down? Now, I tol' you. [*The* CHERUB *starts to come down.*]

STOUT ANGEL

[*To the* CHERUB *with a bone in her throat.*] I tol' you you was too little fo' catfish. What you wanter git a bone in yo' froat fo'? [*She slaps the* CHERUB'S *back.*]

SLENDER ANGEL

[*Leisurely eating a sandwich as she watches the back-slapping.*] What de trouble wid Leonetta?

STOUT ANGEL

She got a catfish bone down her froat. [*To the* CHERUB.] Doggone, I tol' you to eat grinnel instead.

SLENDER ANGEL

Ef'n she do git all dat et, she gonter have de belly-ache.

[13]

STOUT ANGEL

Ain't I tol' her dat? [*To* CHERUB.] Come on now; let go dat bone. [*She slaps* CHERUB's *back again. The bone is dislodged and the* CHERUB *grins her relief.*] Dat's good.

SLENDER ANGEL

[*Comfortingly.*] Now she all right.

STOUT ANGEL

Go on an' play wid yo' cousins. [*The* CHERUB *joins the Cherubs sitting on the embankment. The concurrency of scenes ends here.*] I ain't see you lately, Lily. How you been?

SLENDER ANGEL

Me, I'm fine. I been visitin' my mammy. She waitin' on de welcome table over by de throne of grace.

STOUT ANGEL

She always was pretty holy.

SLENDER ANGEL

Yes, ma'am. She like it dere. I guess de Lawd's took quite a fancy to her.

STOUT ANGEL

Well, dat's natural. I declare yo' mammy one of de finest lady angels I know.

SLENDER ANGEL

She claim you de best one she know.

STOUT ANGEL

Well, when you come right down to it, I suppose we is all pretty near perfec'.

SLENDER ANGEL

Yes, ma'am. Why is dat, Mis' Jenny?

STOUT ANGEL

I s'pose it's caize de Lawd he don' 'low us 'sociatin' wid de devil any mo' so dat dey cain' be no mo' sinnin'.

SLENDER ANGEL

Po' ol' Satan. Whutevah become of him?

STOUT ANGEL

De Lawd put him some place I s'pose.

SLENDER ANGEL

But dey ain't any place but Heaven, is dey?

STOUT ANGEL

De Lawd could make a place, couldn't he?

SLENDER ANGEL

Dat's de truth. Dey's one thing confuses me though.

[15]

STOUT ANGEL

What's dat?

SLENDER ANGEL

I do a great deal of travelin' an' I ain't never come across any place but Heaven anywhere. So if de Lawd kick Satan out of Heaven jest whereat did he go? Dat's my question.

STOUT ANGEL

You bettah let de Lawd keep his own secrets, Lily. De way things is goin' now dey ain't been no sinnin' since dey give dat scamp a kick in de pants. Nowadays Heaven's free of sin an' if a lady wants a little constitutional she kin fly 'til she wing-weary widout gittin' insulted.

SLENDER ANGEL

I was jest a baby when Satan lef'. I don't even 'member what he look like.

STOUT ANGEL

He was jest right fo' a devil. [*An* ARCHANGEL *enters. He is older than the others and wears a white beard. His clothing is much darker than that of the others and his wings a trifle more imposing.*] Good mo'nin', Archangel.

[*Others say good morning.*]

ARCHANGEL

Good mo'nin', folks. I wonder kin I interrup' de fish fry an' give out de Sunday School cyards? [*Cries of "Suttingly!" "Mah goodness, yes"—etc. The marching* CHOIR *stops.*] You kin keep singin' if you want to. Why don' you sing "When de Saints Come Marchin' In?" Seem to me I ain' heard dat lately. [*The* CHOIR *begins "When the Saints Come Marching In," rather softly, but does not resume marching. The* ARCHANGEL *looks off left.*] All right, bring 'em yere. [*A prim looking* WOMAN TEACHER-ANGEL *enters, shepherding ten* BOY *and* GIRL CHERUBS. *The* TEACHER *carries ten beribboned diplomas, which she gives to the* ARCH-ANGEL. *The cherubs are dressed in stiffly starched white suits and dresses, the little girls having enormous ribbons at the backs of their dresses and smaller ones in their hair and on the tips of their wings. They line up in front of the archangel and receive the attention of the rest of the company. The* CHOIR *sings through the ceremony.*] Now den cherubs, why is you yere?

CHILDREN

Because we so good.

ARCHANGEL

Dat's right. Now who de big boss?

CHILDREN

Our dear Lawd.

ARCHANGEL

Dat's right. When you all grow up what you gonter be?

CHILDREN

Holy angels at de throne of grace.

ARCHANGEL

Dat's right. Now, you passed yo' 'xaminations and it gives me great pleasure to hand out de cyards for de whole class. Gineeva Chaproe. [*The* FIRST GIRL CHERUB *goes to him and gets her diploma. The* CHOIR *sings loudly and resumes marching, as the* ARCHANGEL *calls out another name—and presents diplomas.*] Corey Moulter. [SECOND GIRL CHERUB *gets her diploma.*] Nootzie Winebush. [THIRD GIRL CHERUB.] Harriet Prancy. [FOURTH GIRL CHERUB.] I guess you is Brozain Stew't. [*He gives the* FIFTH GIRL CHERUB *the paper. Each of the presentations has been accompanied by hand-clapping from the bystanders.*] Now you boys know yo' own names. Suppose you come yere and help me git dese 'sorted right?

> [BOY CHERUBS *gather about him and receive their diplomas. The little* GIRLS *have scattered about the stage, joining groups of the adult angels.*

The angel GABRIEL *enters. He is bigger and more elaborately winged than even the Archangel, but he is also much younger and beardless. His costume is less conventional than that of the other men, resembling more the Gabriel of the Doré drawings. His appearance causes a flutter among the others. They stop their chattering with the children. The* CHOIR *stops as three or four audible whispers of "Gabriel!" are heard. In a moment the heavenly company is all attention.*]

GABRIEL

[*Lifting his hand.*] Gangway! Gangway for de Lawd God Jehovah!

[*There is a reverent hush and* GOD *enters. He is the tallest and biggest of them all. He wears a white shirt with a white bow tie, a long Prince Albert coat of black alpaca, black trousers and congress gaiters. He looks at the assemblage. There is a pause. He speaks in a rich, bass voice.*]

GOD

Is you been baptized?

OTHERS

[*Chanting.*] Certainly, Lawd.

GOD

Is you been baptized?

OTHERS

Certainly, Lawd.

GOD

[*With the beginning of musical notation.*] Is you been baptized?

OTHERS

[*Now half-singing.*] Certainly, Lawd. Certainly, certainly, certainly, Lawd.

    [*They sing the last two verses with equivalent part division.*]

        Is you been redeemed?
        Certainly, Lawd.
        Is you been redeemed?
        Certainly, Lawd.
        Is you been redeemed?
        Certainly, Lawd. Certainly, certainly, certainly, Lawd.

        Do you bow mighty low?
        Certainly, Lawd.
        Do you bow mighty low?
        Certainly, Lawd.
        Do you bow mighty low?
        Certainly, Lawd. Certainly, certainly, certainly, Lawd.

[*As the last response ends all heads are bowed.
God looks at them for a moment; then lifts His
hand.*]

GOD

Let de fish fry proceed.

[EVERYONE *rises. The* ANGELS *relax and resume
their inaudible conversations. The activity behind the table and about the cauldron is resumed.
Some of the choir members cross to the table and
get sandwiches and cups of the boiled custard.
Three or four of the children in the Sunday
School class and the little girl who had the bone
in her throat affectionately group themselves
about God as he speaks with the Archangel. He
pats their heads, they hang to his coat-tails, etc.*]

ARCHANGEL

Good mo'nin', Lawd.

GOD

Good mo'nin', Deacon. You lookin' pretty spry.

ARCHANGEL

I cain' complain. We just been givin' our cyards to
de chillun.

GOD

Dat's good.

[*A small Cherub, his feet braced against one of
God's shoes is using God's coat-tail as a trapeze.*

One of the COOKS *offers a fish sandwich which* GOD *politely declines.*]

FIRST MAMMY ANGEL

Now, you leave go de Lawd's coat, Herman. You heah me?

GOD

Dat's all right, sister. He jest playin'.

FIRST MAMMY ANGEL

He playin' too rough.
[GOD *picks up the cherub and spanks him good-naturedly. The* CHERUB *squeals with delight and runs to his mother.* GABRIEL *advances to* GOD *with a glass of the custard.*]

GABRIEL

Little b'iled custud, Lawd?

GOD

Thank you very kindly. Dis looks nice.

CUSTARD MAKER

[*Offering a box.*] Ten cent seegar, Lawd?

GOD

[*Taking it.*] Thank you, thank you. How de fish fry goin'? [*Ad lib. cries of* "O. K. Lawd," "Fine an' *dandy, Lawd," "De best one yit, Lawd," etc. To the choir.*] How you shouters gittin' on?

CHOIR LEADER

We been marchin' and singin' de whole mo'nin'.

GOD

I heerd you. You gittin' better all de time. You gittin' as good as de one at de throne. Why don' you give us one dem ol' time jump-ups?

CHOIR LEADER

Anythin' you say, Lawd. [*To the others.*] "So High!"
[*The* CHOIR *begins to sing "So High You Can't Get Over It." They sing softly, but do not march. An* ANGEL *offers his cigar to* GOD *from which He can light His own.*]

GOD

No, thanks. I'm gonter save dis a bit.
[*He puts the cigar in his pocket and listens to the singers a moment. Then he sips his custard. After the second sip, a look of displeasure comes on his face.*]

GABRIEL

What's de matter, Lawd?

GOD

[*Sipping again.*] I ain't jest sure, yit. Dey's something 'bout dis custahd. [*Takes another sip.*]

CUSTARD MAKER

Ain't it all right, Lawd?

GOD

It don't seem seasoned jest right. You make it?

CUSTARD MAKER

Yes, Lawd. I put everythin' in it like I allus do. It's supposed to be perfec'.

GOD

Yeah. I kin taste de eggs and de cream and de sugar. [*Suddenly.*] I know what it is. It needs jest a little bit mo' firmament.

CUSTARD MAKER

Dey's firmament in it, Lawd.

GOD

Maybe, but it ain' enough.

CUSTARD MAKER

It's all we had, Lawd. Dey ain't a drap in de jug.

GOD

Dat's all right. I'll jest r'ar back an' pass a miracle.
[CHOIR *stops singing.*] Let it be some firmament! An'
when I say let it be some firmament, I don't want jest
a little bitty dab o' firmament caize I'm sick an' tired
of runnin' out of it when we need it. Let it be a whole
mess of firmament! [*The stage has become misty until*
GOD *and the heavenly company are obscured. As he*
finishes the speech there is a burst of thunder. As the
stage grows darker.] Dat's de way I like it.

> [*Murmurs from the others; "Dat's a lot of firma-*
> *ment." "My, dat is firmament!" "Look to me*
> *like he's created rain," etc.*]

FIRST MAMMY ANGEL

[*When the stage is dark.*] Now, look Lawd, dat's
too much firmament. De Cherubs is gettin' all wet.

SECOND MAMMY ANGEL

Look at my Carlotta, Lawd. She's soaked to de skin.
Dat's *plenty* too much firmament.

GOD

Well, 'co'se we don't want de chillun to ketch cold.
Can't you dreen it off?

GABRIEL

Dey's no place to dreen it, Lawd.

FIRST MAMMY ANGEL

Why don't we jest take de babies home, Lawd?

GOD

No, I don' wanta bust up de fish fry. You angels keep quiet an I'll pass another miracle. Dat's always de trouble wid miracles. When you pass one you always gotta r'ar back an' pass another. [*There is a hush.*] Let dere be a place to dreen off dis firmament. Let dere be mountains and valleys an' let dere be oceans an' lakes. An' let dere be rivers and bayous to dreen it off in, too. As a matter of fac' let dere be de earth. An' when dat's done let dere be de sun, an' let it come out and dry my Cherubs' wings.

> [*The lights go up until the stage is bathed in sunlight. On the embankment upstage there is now a waist-high wrought iron railing such as one sees on the galleries of houses in the French quarter of New Orleans. The* CHERUBS *are being examined by their parents and there is an ad lib. murmur of, "You all right, honey?" "You feel better now, Albert?" "Now you all dry, Vangy?" until the* ARCHANGEL, *who has been gazing in awe at the railing, drowns them out.*]

ARCHANGEL

Look yere!

> [*There is a rush to the embankment accompanied by exclamations, "My goodness!" "What's dis?"*

"I declah!" etc. GABRIEL *towers above the group on the middle of the embankment.* GOD *is wrapped in thought, facing the audience. The* CHOIR *resumes singing "So High You Can't Get Over It" softly. The babbling at the balustrade dies away as the people lean over the railing.* GABRIEL *turns and faces* GOD *indicating the earth below the railing with his left hand.*]

GABRIEL

Do you see it, Lawd?

GOD

[*Quietly, without turning his head upstage.*] Yes, Gabriel.

GABRIEL

Looks mighty nice, Lawd.

GOD

Yes.
   [GABRIEL *turns and looks over the railing.*]

GABRIEL

[*Gazing down.*] Yes, suh. Dat'd make mighty nice farming country. Jest look at dat South forty over dere. You ain't going to let dat go to waste is you, Lawd? Dat would be a pity an' a shame.

GOD

[*Not turning.*] It's a good earth. [GOD *turns, room is made for him beside* GABRIEL *on the embankment.*] Yes. I ought to have somebody to enjoy it. [*He turns, facing the audience. The others, save for the choir who are lined up in two rows of six on an angle up right, continue to look over the embankment.*] Gabriel! [GOD *steps down from the embankment two paces.*]

GABRIEL

[*Joining him.*] Yes, Lawd.

GOD

Gabriel, I'm goin' down dere.

GABRIEL

Yes, Lawd.

GOD

I want you to be my working boss yere while I'm gone.

GABRIEL

Yes, Lawd.

GOD

You know dat matter of dem two stars?

GABRIEL

Yes, Lawd.

GOD

Git dat fixed up! You know dat sparrow dat fell a little while ago? 'Tend to dat, too.

GABRIEL

Yes, Lawd.

GOD

I guess dat's about all. I'll be back Saddy. [*To the* CHOIR.] Quiet, angels. [*The* CHOIR *stops singing. Those on the embankment circle down stage.* GOD *goes to embankment. Turns and faces the company.*] I'm gonter pass one more miracle. You all gonter help me an' not make a soun' caize it's one of de most impo'tant miracles of all. [*Nobody moves.* GOD *turns, facing the sky and raises his arms above his head.*] Let there be man.

> [*There is growing roll of thunder as stage grows dark. The* CHOIR *bursts into "Hallelujah," and continues until the lights go up on the next scene.*]

SCENE III

Enclosing the stage is a heterogeneous cluster of cottonwood, camphor, live oak and sycamore trees, youpon and turkey berry bushes, with their purple and red berries, sprays of fern-like indigo fiera and splashes of various Louisiana flowers. In the middle of the stage,

*disclosed when the mistiness at rise grows into warm
sunlight, stands* ADAM. *He is a puzzled man of 30, of
medium height, dressed in the clothing of the average
field hand. He is bare-headed. In the distance can be
heard the choir continuing. "Bright Mansions Above."
A bird begins to sing.* ADAM *smiles and turns to look
at the source of this novel sound. He senses his strength
and raises his forearms, his fists clenched. With his
left hand he carefully touches the muscles of his upper
right arm. He smiles again, realizing his power. He
looks at his feet which are stretched wide apart. He
stamps once or twice and now almost laughs in his
enjoyment. Other birds begin trilling and* ADAM *glances
up joyfully toward the foliage.* GOD *enters.*

GOD

Good mo'nin', Son.

ADAM

[*With a little awe.*] Good mo'nin', Lawd.

GOD

What's yo' name, Son?

ADAM

Adam.

GOD

Adam which?

ADAM

[*Frankly, after a moment's puzzled groping.*] Jest Adam, Lawd.

GOD

Well, Adam, how dey treatin' you? How things goin'?

ADAM

Well, Lawd, you know it's kind of a new line of wukk.

GOD

You'll soon get de hang of it. You know yo' kind of a new style with me.

ADAM

Oh, I guess I'm gonter make out all right soon as I learn de ropes.

GOD

Yes, I guess you will. Yo' a nice job.

ADAM

Yes, Lawd.

GOD

Dey's jest one little thing de matter with you. Did you notice it?

ADAM

Well, now you mentioned it, Lawd, I kind of thought dey was somethin' wrong.

[31]

GOD

Yes suh, you ain't quite right. Adam, you need a family. De reason for dat is in yo' heart you is a family man. [*Flicking the ash off his cigar.*] I'd say dat was de main trouble at de moment.

ADAM

[*Smiling.*] Yes sir. [*His smile fades and he is puzzled again.*] At de same time—dey's one thing puzzlin' me, Lawd. Could I ask you a question?

GOD

Why, certainly, Adam.

ADAM

Lawd, jest what *is* a family?

GOD

I'm gonter show you. [*Indicates a spot.*] Jest lie down dere, Adam. Make out like you was goin' to slumber.

ADAM

[*Gently.*] Yes, Lawd.
[*He lies down.* GOD *stands beside him and as he raises his arms above his head the lights go down. In the darkness* GOD *speaks.*]

GOD

EVE. [*Lights go up.* EVE *is standing beside* ADAM. *She is about twenty-six, and quite pretty. She is dressed like a country girl. Her gingham dress is quite new and clean.* GOD *is now at the other side of the stage, looking at them critically.* EVE *looks at* ADAM *in timid wonder and slowly turns her head until she meets the glance of* GOD. ADAM *stands beside* EVE. *They gaze at each other for a moment.* GOD *smiles.*] Now you all right, Eve. [ADAM *and* EVE *face him.*] Now I'll tell you what I'm gonter do. I'm gonter put you in charge here. I'm gonter give you de run of dis whole garden. Eve, you take care of dis man an' Adam you take care of dis woman. You belong to each other. I don' want you to try to do too much caize yo' both kind of experiment wid me an' I ain't sho' whether you could make it. You two jest enjoy yo'self. Drink de water from de little brooks an' de wine from de grapes an' de berries, an' eat de food dat's hangin' for you in de trees. [*He pauses, startled by a painful thought.*] Dat is, in all but one tree. [*He pauses. Then, not looking at them.*] You know what I mean, my children?

ADAM AND EVE

Yes, Lawd. [*They slowly turn their heads left, toward the branches of an offstage tree. Then they look back at* GOD.]

ADAM

Thank you, Lawd.

EVE

Thank you, Lawd.

GOD

I gotter be gittin' along now. I got a hund'ed thou-san' things to do 'fo' you take yo' nex' breath. Enjoy yo'selves——

[GOD *exits.*]

[ADAM *and* EVE *stand looking after Him for a moment, then each looks down and watches their hands meet and clasp.*]

[*After a moment they lift their heads slowly until they are again gazing at the tree.*]

EVE

Adam.

ADAM

[*Looking at the tree, almost in terror.*] What?

EVE

[*Softly as she too continues to look at the tree.*] Adam.

[*The* CHOIR *begins singing "Turn You Round" and as the lights go down the* CHOIR *continues until there is blackness. The* CHOIR *suddenly stops. The following scene is played in the dark-ness.*]

MR. DESHEE'S VOICE

Now, I s'pose you chillun know what happened after God made Adam 'n' Eve. Do you?

[34]

FIRST GIRL'S VOICE

I know, Mr. Deshee.

MR. DESHEE'S VOICE

Jest a minute, Randolph. Didn't I tell you you gotta tell yo' mammy let yo' sister bring you. Carlisle, take way dat truck he's eatin'. You sit by him, see kin you keep him quiet. Now, den, Myrtle what happened?

FIRST GIRL'S VOICE

Why, den dey ate de fo'bidden fruit and den dey got driv' out de garden.

MR. DESHEE'S VOICE

An' den what happened?

FIRST GIRL'S VOICE

Den dey felt ver bad.

MR. DESHEE'S VOICE

I don' mean how dey feel, I mean how dey do. Do dey have any children or anything like dat?

FIRST GIRL'S VOICE

Oh, yes, suh, dey have Cain 'n' Abel.

MR. DESHEE'S VOICE

Dat's right, dey have Cain an' Abel.

BOY'S VOICE

Dat was a long time after dey got married, wasn't it, Mr. Deshee? My mammy say it was a hund'ed years.

MR. DESHEE'S VOICE

Well, nobody kin be so sure. As I tol' you befo' dey was jest beginnin' to be able to tell de time an' nobody was any too sure 'bout anythin' even den. So de bes' thing to do is jest realize dat de thing happened an' don't bother 'bout how many years it was. Jest remember what I told you about it gittin' dark when you go to sleep an' it bein' light when you wake up. Dat's de way time went by in dem days. One thing we do know an' dat was dis boy Cain was a mean rascal.

[*The lights go up on the next scene.*]

SCENE IV

A roadside.

CAIN, *a husky young Negro, stands over the body of the dead* ABEL. *Both are dressed as laborers.* CAIN *is looking at the body in awe, a rock in his right hand.* GOD *enters.*

GOD

Cain, look what you done to Abel.

CAIN

Lawd, I was min'in' my own business and he come monkeyin' aroun' wit' me. I was wukkin' in de fiel' an' he was sittin' in de shade of de tree. He say "Me, I'd be skeered to git out in dis hot sun. I be 'fraid my brains git cooked. Co'se you ain't got no brains so you ain' in no danger." An' so I up and flang de rock. If it miss 'im all right, an' if it hit 'im, all right. Dat's de way I feel.

GOD

All right, but I'm yere to tell you dat's called a crime. When de new Judge is done talkin' to you you'll be draggin' a ball and chain de rest of yo' life.

CAIN

Well, what'd he want to come monkeyin' aroun' me fo' den? I was jest plowin', min'in' my own business, and not payin' him no min', and yere he come makin' me de fool. I'd bust anybody what make me de fool.

GOD

Well, I ain't sayin' you right an' I ain't sayin' you wrong. But I do say was I you I'd jest git myself down de road 'til I was clean out of de county. An' you better take an' git married an' settle down an' raise some chillun. Dey ain't nothin' to make a man fo'git his troubles like raisin' a family. Now, you better git.

[37]

CAIN

Yessuh.

[CAIN *walks off.*]

[GOD *watches him from the forestage and as the lights begin to dim looks off. The* CHOIR *begins "Run, Sinner, Run."*]

GOD

Adam an' Eve you better try again. You better have Seth an' a lot mo' chillun.

[*There is darkness. The* CHOIR *continues until the lights go up on the next scene.*]

SCENE V

CAIN *is discovered walking on an unseen treadmill. A middle distance of trees, hillsides and shrubbery passes him on an upper treadmill. Behind is the blue sky He stops under the branches of a tree to look at a sign on a fence railing. Only half the tree is visible on the stage. The sign reads,* "NOD PARISH. COUNTY LINE."

CAIN

[*Sitting down with a sigh of relief under the tree.*] At las'! Phew! [*Wipes his forehead with a handkerchief.*] Feels like I been walkin' fo'ty years. [*He looks back.*] Well, dey cain' git me now. Now I kin raise a

[38]

fam'ly. [*An idea occurs to him, and suddenly he begins looking right and left.*] Well, I'll be hit by a mule! Knock me down for a trustin' baby! Where I gonter git dat fam'ly? Dat preacher fooled me. [*He is quite dejected.*] Doggone!

CAIN'S GIRL

[*Off stage.*] Hello, Country Boy!

[CAIN *glances up to the offstage branches of the tree.*]

CAIN

Hey-ho, Good lookin'! Which way is it to town?

CAIN'S GIRL

[*Off stage.*] What you tryin' to do? You tryin' to mash me? I be doggone if it ain't gittin' so a gal cain't hardly leave de house 'out some of dese fast men ain' passin' remarks at her.

CAIN

I ain' passin' remarks.

CAIN'S GIRL

[*Off stage.*] If I thought you was tryin' to mash me, I'd call de police an' git you tooken to de first precinct.

CAIN

Look yere, gal, I ast you a question, an' if you don' answer me I'm gonter bend you 'cross my pants an' burn you up.

CAIN'S GIRL

[*Off stage.*] I'm comin' down.
  [CAIN *takes his eyes from the tree.*]

CAIN

Yes, an' you better hurry.
  [CAIN'S GIRL *enters. She is as large as* CAIN, *wickedly pretty, and somewhat flashily dressed. She smiles at* CAIN.]

CAIN'S GIRL

I bet you kin handle a gal mean wid dem big stout arms of your'n. I sho' would hate to git you mad at me, Country Boy.

CAIN

[*Smiling.*] Come yere. [*She goes a little closer to him.*] Don't be 'fraid, I ain' so mean.

CAIN'S GIRL

You got two bad lookin' eyes. I bet yo' hot coffee 'mong de women folks.

CAIN

I ain' never find out. What was you doin' in dat tree?

CAIN'S GIRL

Jest coolin' myself in de element.

[40]

CAIN

Is you a Nod Parish gal?

CAIN'S GIRL

Bo'n an' bred.

CAIN

You know yo' kinda pretty.

CAIN'S GIRL

Who tol' you dat?

CAIN

Dese yere two bad eyes of mine.

CAIN'S GIRL

I bet you say dat to everybody all de way down de road.

CAIN

Comin' down dat road I didn't talk to nobody.

CAIN'S GIRL

Where you boun' for, Beautiful?

CAIN

I'm jest seein' de country. I thought I might settle down yere fo' a spell. You live wit' yo' people?

CAIN'S GIRL

Co'se I does.

[41]

CAIN

'Spose dey'd like to take in a boarder?

CAIN'S GIRL

Be nice if dey would, wouldn' it?

CAIN

I think so. You got a beau?

CAIN'S GIRL

Huh-uh!

CAIN

[*Smiling.*] You has *now.*

CAIN'S GIRL

I guess—I guess if you wanted to kiss me an' I tried to stop you, you could pretty nearly crush me wit' dem stout arms.

CAIN

You wouldn't try too much, would you?

CAIN'S GIRL

Maybe for a little while.

CAIN

An' den what?

CAIN'S GIRL

Why don' we wait an' see?

CAIN

When would dat be?

CAIN'S GIRL

Tonight. After supper. Think you kin walk a little
further now, City Boy?

CAIN

Yeh, I ain't so weary now.
  [*She takes his hand.*]

CAIN'S GIRL

What yo' name? [*Takes his arm.*]

CAIN

Cain.

CAIN'S GIRL

Then I'm Cain's Gal. Come on, honey, an' meet de
folks.
  [*They exit.*]
  [*The choir is heard singing "You Better Mind,"
    as* GOD *enters.* GOD *watches the vanished* CAIN
    and his girl.]

GOD

[*After shaking his head.*] Bad business. I don' like
de way things is goin' atall.
  [*The stage is darkened.*]
  [*The* CHOIR *continues singing until the lights go
    up on the next scene.*]

Scene VI

God's *private office in Heaven. It is a small room, framed by tableau curtains. A large window up center looks out on the sky. There is a battered roll-top desk. On the wall next to the window is a framed religious oleograph with a calendar attached to it underneath. A door is at the left. A hat rack is on the wall above the door. There are two or three cheap pine chairs beside the window, and beyond the door. In front of the desk is an old swivel armchair which creaks every time* God *leans back in it. The desk is open and various papers are stuck in the pigeonholes. Writing implements, etc. are on the desk. On a shelf above the desk is a row of law books. A cuspidor is near the desk, and a waste basket by it. The general atmosphere is that of the office of a Negro lawyer in a Louisiana town. As the lights go up* God *takes a fresh cigar from a box on the desk and begins puffing it without bothering to light it. There is no comment on this minor miracle fom* Gabriel *who is sitting in one of the chairs with a pencil and several papers in his hand. The singing becomes pianissimo.*

GABRIEL

[*Looking at the papers.*] Well, I guess dat's about all de impo'tant business this mornin', Lawd.

GOD

How 'bout dat Cherub over to Archangel Montgomery's house?

GABRIEL

Where do dey live, Lawd?
[*The singing stops.*]

GOD

Dat little two story gold house, over by de pearly gates.

GABRIEL

Oh, *dat* Montgomery. I thought you was referrin' to de ol' gentleman. Oh, yeh. [*He sorts through the papers and finds one he is looking for.*] Yere it 'tis. [*Reads.*] "Cherub Christina Montgomery; wings is moltin' out of season an' nobody knows what to do."

GOD

Well, now, take keer of dat. You gotter be more careful, Gabe.

GABRIEL

Yes, Lawd.
[*Folds the papers and puts them in a pocket. GOD turns to his desk, takes another puff or two of the cigar, and with a pencil, begins checking off items on a sheet of paper before him. His back is turned toward GABRIEL. GABRIEL takes his trumpet from the hat rack and burnishes it with*

[45]

*his robe. He then wets his lips and puts the
mouthpiece to his mouth.*]

GOD

[*Without turning around.*] Now, watch yo'self,
Gabriel.

GABRIEL

I wasn't goin' to blow, Lawd. I jest do dat every
now an' den so I can keep de feel of it.

[*He leans trumpet against the wall.* GOD *picks up
the papers and swings his chair around toward*
GABRIEL.]

GOD

What's dis yere about de moon?

GABRIEL

[*Suddenly remembering.*] Oh! De moon people
say it's beginnin' to melt a little, on 'count caize de sun's
so hot.

GOD

It's goin' 'roun' 'cordin' to schedule, ain't it?

GABRIEL

Yes, Lawd.

GOD

Well, tell 'em to stop groanin'. Dere's nothin' de
matter wid dat moon. Trouble is so many angels is
flyin' over dere on Saddy night. Dey git to beatin' dere

wings when dey dancin' an' dat makes de heat. Tell dem dat from now on dancin' 'roun' de moon is sinnin'. Dey got to stop it. Dat'll cool off de moon. [*He swings back and puts the paper on the desk. He leans back in the chair comfortably, his hands clasped behind his head.*] Is dere anythin' else you ought to remin' me of?

GABRIEL

De prayers, Lawd.

GOD

[*Puzzled, slowly swinging chair around again.*] De prayers?

GABRIEL

From mankind. You know, down on de earth.

GOD

Oh, yeh, de poor little earth. Bless my soul, I almos' forgot about dat. Mus' be three or four hund'ed years since I been down dere. I wasn't any too pleased wid dat job.

GABRIEL

[*Laughing.*] You know you don' make mistakes, Lawd.

GOD

[*Soberly, with introspective detachment.*] So dey tell me. [*He looks at* GABRIEL, *then through the window again.*] So dey tell me. I fin' I kin be displeased though, an' I was displeased wid de mankind I las' seen. Maybe I ought to go down dere agin—I need a little holiday.

GABRIEL

Might do you good, Lawd.

GOD

I think I will. I'll go down an' walk de earth agin an' see how dem poor humans is makin' out. What time is it, by de sun an' de stars?

GABRIEL

[*Glancing out of the window.*] Jest exactly half-past, Lawd.

[GOD *is taking his hat and stick from the hat rack.*]

GOD

[*Opening the door.*] Well, take keer o' yo'self. I'll be back Saddy. [*He exits.*]

[*The stage is darkened. The* CHOIR *begins "Dere's no Hidin' Place," and continues until the lights go up on the next scene.*]

SCENE VII

GOD *is walking along a country road. He stops to listen. Church bells are heard in the distance.*

GOD

Dat's nice. Nice an' quiet. Dat's de way I like Sunday to be. [*The sound is broken by a shrill voice of*

[48]

a girl. It is ZEBA *singing a "blues."*] Now, dat ain't so good. [GOD *resumes his walk and the upper tread-mill brings on a tree stump on which* ZEBA *is sitting. She is accompanying her song with a ukulele.* GOD *and the treadmills stop. When the stump reaches the center of the stage, it is seen that* ZEBA *is a rouged and extremely flashily dressed chippy of about eighteen.*] Stop dat!

ZEBA

What's de matter wid you, Country Boy? Pull up yo' pants. [*She resumes singing.*]

GOD

Stop dat!

ZEBA

[*Stops again.*] Say, listen to me, Banjo Eyes. What right you got to stop a lady enjoyin' herself?

GOD

Don't you know dis is de Sabbath? Da's no kin' o' song to sing on de Lawd's day.

ZEBA

Who care 'bout de Lawd's day, anymo'? People jest use Sunday now to git over Saddy.

GOD

You a awful sassy little girl.

[49]

ZEBA

I come fum sassy people! We even speak mean of de dead.

GOD

What's yo' name?

ZEBA

[*Flirtatiously.*] "What's my name?" Ain't you de ol'-time gal hunter! Fust, "What's my name?" den I s'pose, what would it be like if you tried to kiss me? You preachers' is de debbils.

GOD

I ain't aimin' to touch you daughter. [*A sudden sternness frightens* ZEBA. *She looks at him sharply.*] What is yo' name?

ZEBA

Zeba.

GOD

Who's yo' fam'ly?

ZEBA

I'm de great-great gran' daughter of Seth.

GOD

Of Seth? But Seth was a good man.

ZEBA

Yeh, he too good, he die of holiness.

GOD

An' yere's his little gran' daughter reekin' wid cologne. Ain't nobody ever tol' you yo' on de road to Hell?

ZEBA

[*Smiling.*] Sho' dat's what de preacher say. Exceptin' of course, I happens to know dat I'm on de road to de picnic groun's, an' at de present time I'm waitin' to keep a engagement wid my sweet papa. He don' like people talkin' to me.

[CAIN THE SIXTH *enters. He is a young buck, wearing a "box" coat and the other flashy garments of a Rampart Street swell.*]

CAIN THE SIXTH

Hello, sugah! [*He crosses in front of* GOD *and faces* ZEBA.] Hello, mamma! Sorry I'm late baby, but de gals in de barrel-house jest wouldn't let me go. Doggone, one little wirehead swore she'd tear me down.

[ZEBA *smiles and takes his hand.*]

GOD

What's yo' name, son?

CAIN THE SIXTH

[*Contemptuously; without turning.*] Soap 'n water, Country Boy.

GOD

[*Sternly.*] What's yo' name, son?
  [CAIN *slowly turns and for a moment his manner
  is civil.*]

CAIN THE SIXTH

Cain the Sixth.

GOD

I was afraid so.

CAIN THE SIXTH

[*His impudence returning.*] You a new preacher?

GOD

Where you live?

CAIN THE SIXTH

Me, I live mos' any place.

GOD

Yes, an' you gonter see dem all. Is de udder young
men all like you?

CAIN THE SIXTH

[*Smiling.*] De gals don' think so.
  [*He turns towards* ZEBA *again, picks her up and
  sits on the stump with the laughing* ZEBA *on his
  lap.*]

[52]

ZEBA

Dey ain't nobody in de worl' like my honey-cake.
[CAIN *kisses her and she resumes her song.*]
[GOD *watches them.* ZEBA *finishes a verse of the song and begins another softly.* CAIN THE SIXTH's *eyes have been closed during the singing.*]

CAIN THE SIXTH

[*His eyes closed.*] Is de preacher gone?
[ZEBA *looks quickly at* GOD *without seeing him, and then looks off. She stops the song.*]

ZEBA

Yeh, I guess he walks fast.
[CAIN *pushes her off his lap and rises.*]

CAIN THE SIXTH

[*With acid sweetness.*] Dey tell me las' night you was talkin' to a creeper man, baby.

ZEBA

Why, you know dey ain't nobody in de world fo' me but you.

CAIN THE SIXTH

[*Smiling.*] I know dey ain't. I even got dat guaranteed. [*Takes a revolver from his pocket.*] See dat, baby?

[53]

ZEBA

Sho' I see it, honey.

CAIN THE SIXTH

Dat jest makes me positive. [*Puts the gun back.*]

ZEBA

[*Pushing him back on the stump.*] You don' wanter believe dem stories, papa.

CAIN THE SIXTH

[*With sinister lightness.*] No, I didn't believe dem, baby. Co'se dat big gorilla, Flatfoot, from de other side of de river *is* in town ag'in.

ZEBA

Dat don' mean nothin'. Flatfoot ain't nothin' to me.

CAIN THE SIXTH

[*Sitting again.*] Co'se he ain't. Go 'head, sing some mo', baby.

[ZEBA *resumes singing.*]

GOD

Bad business. [*The treadmills start turning.* GOD *resumes his walk.* ZEBA, *still singing, and* CAIN THE SIXTH *recede with the landscape.* GOD *is again alone on the country road. There is a twitter of birds.* GOD *looks up and smiles.*] De birds is goin' 'bout dere business, all right. [*A patch of flowers goes by, black-eyed Susans, conspicuously.*] How you flowers makin' out? [*Children's voices answer, "We O. K., Lawd."*] Yes, an' you looks very pretty. [*Children's voices: "Thank you, Lawd." The flowers pass out of sight.*] It's only de human bein's makes me downhearted. Yere's as nice a Sunday as dey is turnin' out anywhere, an' nobody makin' de right use of it. [*Something ahead of him attracts his attention. His face brightens.*] Well, now dis is mo' like it. Now dat's nice to see people prayin'. It's a wonder dey don' do it in de church. But I fin' I don' min' it if dey do it outdoors.

> [*A group of five adult Negroes and a boy on their knees in a semicircle, appears. The treadmills stop. The* BOY, *his head bent, swings his hands rhythmically up to his head three or four times. There is a hush.*]

GAMBLER

Oh, Lawd, de smoke-house is empty. Oh, Lawd, lemme git dem groceries. Oh, Lawd, lemme see dat little *six*. [*He casts the dice.*] Wham! Dere she is, frien's.

> [*Exclamations from the others: "Well damn my eyes!" "Doggone, dat's de eighth pass he make." "For God's sake, can't you ever crap?" etc. The* BOY *is picking up the money.*]

GOD

Gamblin'! [*Looks over the group's shoulders.*] An' wid frozen dice!

BOY GAMBLER

Dey's a dolla' 'n' a half talkin' fo' me. How much you want of it, Riney?

FIRST GAMBLER

I take fo' bits. Wait a minute. Mebbe I take a little mo'. [*He counts some money in his hand.*]

SECOND GAMBLER

[*Glancing up at* GOD.] Hello, Liver Lips. [*To the others.*] Looka ol' Liver Lips.

> [*The others look up and laugh good-naturedly, re-*
> *peating "Liver Lips."*]

FIRST GAMBLER

Ain't his pockets high from de goun'? Ol' High Pockets.

> [*The others keep saying "Ole Liver Lips." "Ol'*
> *Liver Lips don't like to see people dicin'." "Dat's*
> *a good name, 'High Pockets.'"*]

BOY GAMBLER

[*To others.*] Come on, you gonter fade me or not?

> [GOD *seizes the boy's ears and drags him to his*
> *feet. The others do not move, but watch,*
> *amused.*]

GOD

Come yere, son. Why, yo' jest a little boy. Gamblin' an' sinnin'. [GOD *looks at the boy's face.*] You been chewin' tobacco, too, like you was yo' daddy. [GOD *sniffs.*] An' you been drinkin' sonny-kick-mammy-wine. You oughta be 'shamed. [*To the others.*] An' you gamblers oughta be 'shamed, leadin' dis boy to sin.

FIRST GAMBLER

He de bes' crap shooter in town, mister.

GOD

I'm gonter tell his mammy. I bet she don' know 'bout dis.

FIRST GAMBLER

No, she don' know. [*The others laugh.*] She don' know anythin'.

SECOND GAMBLER

Das de God's truth.

FIRST GAMBLER

See kin you beat 'im, High Pockets. Dey's a dolla' open yere.

GOD

I ain't gonter beat 'im. I'm gonter teach 'im. I may have to teach you all.

[*He starts walking from them. The* BOY *sticks out his tongue the moment* GOD's *back is turned.*]

BOY GAMBLER

If you fin' my mammy you do mo'n I kin. Come on, gamblers, see kin you gimme a little action. Who wants any part of dat dollar?

[*The treadmill carries them off. The* FIRST GAMBLER *is heard saying: "I'll take anoder two bits," and the others, "Gimme a dime's wo'th," "I ain't only got fifteen cents left," etc. as they disappear.*]

GOD

[*Walking.*] Where's dat little boy's home? [*The front of a shanty appears and* GOD *stops in front of the door.*] Yere's de place. It ain't any too clean, either. [*Knocks on the door with his cane.*]

VOICE IN SHANTY

Who dar?

GOD

Never you min' who's yere. Open de door.

VOICE IN SHANTY

You gotta search warrant?

GOD

I don' need one.

[58]

VOICE IN SHANTY

Who you wanter see?

GOD

I wanter see de mammy of de little gamblin' boy.

VOICE IN SHANTY

You mean little Johnny Rucker?

GOD

Dat may be his name.

VOICE IN SHANTY

Well, Mrs. Rucker ain't home.

GOD

Where's she at?

VOICE IN SHANTY

Who, Mrs. Rucker?

GOD

You heerd me.

VOICE IN SHANTY

Oh, she run away las' night wid a railroad man. She's eloped.

GOD

Where's Rucker?

VOICE IN SHANTY

He's flat under de table. He so drunk he cain't move.

GOD

Who are you?

[59]

I'se jest a fren' an' neighbor. I come in las' night to de party, an' everybody in yere's dead drunk but me. De only reason I kin talk is I drank some new white mule I made myself, an' it burn my throat so I cain't drink no mo'. You got any mo' questions?

GOD

Not for you.

[*The shanty begins to move off as* GOD *starts walking again.*]

VOICE IN SHANTY

Good riddance, I say.

[*Shanty disappears.*]

GOD

Dis ain't gittin' me nowheres. All I gotta say dis yere mankind I been peoplin' my earth wid sho' ain't much. [*He stops and looks back.*] I got good min' to wipe 'em all off an' people de earth wid angels. No. Angels is all right, singin' an' playin' an' flyin' around, but dey ain't much on workin' de crops and buildin' de levees. No, suh, mankind's jest right for my earth, if he wasn't so doggone sinful. I'd rather have my earth peopled wit' a bunch of channel catfish, dan I would mankin' an' his sin. I jest cain't stan' sin.

[*He is about to resume his walk when* NOAH *enters.* NOAH *is dressed like a country preacher.*

His coat is of the "hammer-tail" variety. He carries a prayer book under his arm.]

NOAH

Mo'nin', brother.

GOD

Mo'nin', brother. I declare you look like a good man.

NOAH

I try to be, brother. I'm de preacher yere. I don't think I seen you to de meetin'.

[*They resume walking.*]

GOD

I jest come to town a little while ago an' I been pretty busy.

NOAH

Yeh, mos' everybody say dey's pretty busy dese days. Dey so busy dey cain't come to meetin'. It seem like de mo' I preaches de mo' people ain't got time to come to church. I ain't hardly got enough members to fill up de choir. I gotta do de preachin' an' de bassin' too.

GOD

Is dat a fac'?

NOAH

Yes, suh, brother. Everybody is mighty busy, gamblin', good-timin', an' goin' on. You jest wait, though.

When Gabriel blow de horn you gonter fin' dey got plenty of time to punch chunks down in Hell. Yes, suh.

GOD

Seems a pity. Dey all perfec'ly healthy?

NOAH

Oh, dey healthy, all right. Dey jest all lazy, and mean, and full of sin. You look like a preacher, too, brother.

GOD

Well, I am, in a way.

NOAH

You jest passin' through de neighborhood?

GOD

Yes. I wanted to see how things was goin' in yo' part of de country, an' I been feelin' jest 'bout de way you do. It's enough to discourage you.

NOAH

Yes, but I gotta keep wres'lin' wid 'em. Where you boun' for right now, brother?

GOD

I was jest walkin' along. I thought I might stroll on to de nex' town.

NOAH

Well, dat's a pretty good distance. I live right yere. [*He stops walking.*] Why don' you stop an' give us de pleasure of yo' comp'ny for dinner? I believe my ol' woman has kilt a chicken.

GOD

Why, dat's mighty nice of you, brother. I don' believe I caught yo' name.

NOAH

Noah, jest brother Noah. Dis is my home, brother. Come right in.

[GOD *and* NOAH *start walking towards Noah's house which is just coming into view on the treadmill.*]

[*The stage darkens, the* CHOIR *sings "Feastin' Table," and when the lights go up again, the next scene is disclosed.*]

SCENE VIII

Interior of Noah's house. The ensemble suggests the combination living-dining room in a fairly prosperous Negro's cabin. Clean white curtains hang at the window. A table and chairs are in the center of the room. There is a cheerful checked tablecloth on the table, and on the wall, a framed, highly colored picture reading "God Bless Our Home."

> [NOAH'S WIFE, *an elderly Negress, simply and neatly dressed,* GOD *and* NOAH *are discovered grouped about the table.*]

NOAH

Company, darlin'. (*Noah's wife takes Noah's and God's hats.*) Dis gemman's a preacher, too. He's jest passin' through de country.

GOD

Good mo'nin', sister.

NOAH'S WIFE

Good mo'nin'. You jest ketch me when I'm gittin' dinner ready. You gonter stay with us?

GOD

If I ain't intrudin'. Brother Noah suggested—

NOAH'S WIFE

You set right down yere. I got a chicken in de pot an' it'll be ready in 'bout five minutes. I'll go out de back an' call Shem, Ham 'n' Japheth. [*To* GOD.] Dey's our sons. Dey live right acrost de way but always have Sunday dinner wid us. You mens make yo'selves comf'table.

GOD

Thank you, thank you very kindly.

NOAH

You run along, we all right.
[GOD *and* NOAH *seat themselves.* NOAH's WIFE *exits.*]

GOD

You got a fine wife, Brother Noah.

NOAH

She pretty good woman.

GOD

Yes, suh, an' you got a nice little home. Have a ten cent seegar? [GOD *offers him one.*]

NOAH

Thank you, much obliged.
[*Both men lean back restfully in their chairs.*]

GOD

Jest what seems to be de main trouble 'mong mankind, Noah?

NOAH

Well, it seems to me de main trouble is dat de whol' distric' is wide open. Now you know dat makes fo' loose livin'. Men folks spen's all dere time fightin', loafin' an' gamblin', an' makin' bad likker.

GOD

What about de women?

NOAH

De women is worse dan de men. If dey ain't makin' love powder dey out beg, borrow an' stealin' money for policy tickets. Doggone, I come in de church Sunday 'fo' las' 'bout an' hour befo' de meetin' was to start, and dere was a woman stealin' de altar cloth. She was goin' to hock it. Dey ain't got no moral sense. Now you take dat case las' month, over in East Putney. Case of dat young Willy Roback.

GOD

What about him?

NOAH

Dere is a boy sebenteen years old. Doggone, if he didn't elope with his aunt. Now, you know, dat kin' of goin' on is bad fo' a neighborhood.

GOD

Terrible, terrible.

NOAH

Yes, suh. Dis use' to be a nice, decent community. I been doin' my best to preach de Word, but seems like every time I preach de place jest goes a little mo' to de dogs. De good Lawd only knows what's gonter happen.

GOD

Dat is de truth.

[*There is a pause. Each puffs his cigar.*]

[*Suddenly* NOAH *grasps his knee, as if it were paining him, and twists his foot.*]

NOAH

Huh!

GOD

What's de matter?

NOAH

I jest got a twitch. My buck-aguer I guess. Every now and den I gets a twitch in de knee. Might be a sign of rain.

GOD

That's just what it is. Noah, what's de mos' rain you ever had 'round dese parts?

NOAH

Well, de water come down fo' six days steady last April an' de ribber got so swole it bust down de levee up 'bove Freeport. Raise cain all de way down to de delta.

GOD

What would you say was it to rain for forty days and forty nights?

NOAH

I'd say dat was a *complete* rain!

[67]

GOD

Noah, you don't know who I is, do you?

NOAH

[*Puzzled.*] Yo' face looks easy, but I don' think I recall de name.

[GOD *rises slowly, and as he reaches his full height there is a crash of lightning, a moment's darkness, and a roll of thunder. It grows light again.* NOAH *is on his knees in front of* GOD.]

I should have known you. I should have seen de glory.

GOD

Dat's all right, Noah. You didn' know who I was.

NOAH

I'm jes' ol' preacher Noah, Lawd, an' I'm yo' servant. I ain' very much, but I'se all I got.

GOD

Sit down, Noah. Don' let me hear you shamin' yo'se'f, caize yo' a good man. [*Timidly* NOAH *waits until* GOD *is seated, and then sits, himself.*] I jest wanted to fin' out if you was good, Noah. Dat's why I'm walkin' de earth in de shape of a natchel man. I wish dey was mo' people like you. But, far as I kin see you and yo' fam'ly is de only respectable people in de worl'.

NOAH

Dey jest all poor sinners, Lawd.

GOD

I know. I am your Lawd. I am a god of wrath and vengeance an' dat's why I'm gonter destroy dis worl'.

NOAH

[*Almost in a whisper. Drawing back.*] Jest as you say, Lawd.

GOD

I ain't gonter destroy you, Noah. You and yo' fam'ly, yo' sheep an' cattle, an' all de udder things dat ain't human I'm gonter preserve. But de rest is gotta go. [*Takes a pencil and a sheet of paper from his pocket.*] Look yere, Noah. [NOAH *comes over and looks over his shoulder.*] I want you to build me a boat. I want you to call it de "Ark," and I want it to look like dis. [*He is drawing on the paper. Continues to write as he speaks.*] I want you to take two of every kind of animal and bird dat's in de country. I want you to take seeds an' sprouts an' everythin' like dat an' put dem on dat Ark, because dere is gonter be all dat rain. Dey's gonter to be a deluge, Noah, an' dey's goin' to be a flood. De levees is gonter bust an' everything dat's fastened down is comin' loose, but it ain't gonter float long, caize I'm gonter make a storm dat'll sink everythin' from a hencoop to a barn. Dey ain't a ship on de sea dat'll be able to fight dat tempest. Dey all got to go. Everythin'. Everythin' in dis pretty worl' I made, except one thing, Noah. You an' yo' fam'ly an' de things I said are going to ride dat storm in de Ark. Yere's de way it's to be. [*He hands* NOAH *the paper.* NOAH *takes it and reads.*]

NOAH

[*Pause. Looks at paper again.*] Yes, suh, dis seems to be complete. Now 'bout the animals, Lawd, you say you want everythin'?

GOD

Two of everythin'.

NOAH

Dat would include jayraffes an' hippopotamusses?

GOD

Everythin' dat is.

NOAH

Dey was a circus in town las' week. I guess I kin fin' dem. Co'se I kin git all de rabbits an' possums an' wil' turkeys easy. I'll sen' de boys out. Hum, I'm jest wonderin'—

GOD

'Bout what?

NOAH

'Bout snakes? Think you'd like snakes, too?

GOD

Certainly, I want snakes.

NOAH

Oh, I kin git snakes, lots of 'em. Co'se, some of 'em's a little dangerous. Maybe I better take a kag of likker, too?

GOD

You kin have a kag of likker.

NOAH

[*Musingly.*] Yes, suh, dey's a awful lot of differ'nt kin's of snakes, come to think about it. Dey's water moccasins, cotton-moufs, rattlers—mus' be a hund'ed kin's of other snakes down in de swamps. Maybe I better take two kags of likker.

GOD

[*Mildly.*] I think de one kag's enough.

NOAH

No. I better take two kags. Besides I kin put one on each side of de boat, an' balance de ship wid dem as well as havin' dem fo' medicinal use.

GOD

You kin put one kag in de middle of de ship.

NOAH

[*Buoyantly.*] Jest as easy to take de two kags, Lawd.

GOD

I think one kag's enough.

NOAH

Yes, Lawd, but you see forty days an' forty nights——
[*There is a distant roll of thunder.*]

GOD

[*Firmly.*] One kag, Noah.

NOAH

Yes, Lawd. One kag.
[*The door in the back opens and* NOAH'S WIFE *enters with a tray of dishes and food.*]

NOAH'S WIFE

Now, den, gen'lemen, if you'll jest draw up cheers.
[*The stage is darkened. The* CHOIR *is heard singing "I Want to Be Ready." They continue in the darkness until the lights go up on the next scene.*]

SCENE IX

In the middle of the stage is the Ark. On the hillside, below the Ark, a dozen or more men and women, townspeople, are watching NOAH, SHEM, HAM *and* JAPHETH *on the deck of the Ark. The three sons are busily nailing boards on the cabin.* NOAH *is smoking a pipe. He wears a silk hat, captain's uniform and a "slicker."*

NOAH

[*To* SHEM.] You, Shem, tote up some ol' rough lumber, don' bring up any planed up lumber, caize dat ain't fo' de main deck.

SHEM

Pretty near supper time, daddy.

NOAH

Maybe 'tis, but I got de feelin' we ought to keep goin'.

FIRST WOMAN

You gonter work all night, Noah, maybe, huh?

NOAH

[*Without looking at her.*] If de sperrit move me.

[73]

SECOND WOMAN

Look yere, Noah, whyn't you give up all dis damn foolishness? Don' you know people sayin' yo' crazy? What you think you doin' anyway?

NOAH

I'se buildin' a Ark. [*Other men and women join those in the foreground.*] Ham, you better stop for a while 'n see whether dey bringin' de animals up all right. [*He looks at his watch.*] Dey ought to be pretty near de foot o' de hill by dis time; if dey ain't you wait fo' dem and bring 'em yo'se'f.

> [HAM *goes down a ladder at the side of the ship and exits during the following scene. The newcomers in group have been speaking to some of the early arrivals.*]

SECOND WOMAN

[*To* THIRD WOMAN, *one of the newcomers.*] No, you don't mean it!

THIRD WOMAN

I do so. Dat's what de talk is in de town.

FIRST MAN

You hear dat, Noah? Dey say yo' ol' lady is tellin' everybody it's gonter rain fo' fo'ty days and fo'ty nights. You know people soon gonter git de idea you *all* crazy.

NOAH

Lot I keer what you think. [*To* JAPHETH.] Straighten up dem boards down dere, Japheth. [*Indicates floor of deck.*]

FIRST MAN

[*To* THIRD WOMAN.] Was I you, I wouldn' go 'round with Mrs. Noah anymore, lady. Fust thing you know you'll be gittin' a hard name, too.

THIRD WOMAN

Don' I know?

SECOND WOMAN

A lady cain't be too partic'lar dese days.
  [ZEBA *and* FLATFOOT, *a tall, black, wicked-looking buck, enter, their arms around each other's waist.*]

ZEBA

Dere it is baby. Was I lyin'?

FLATFOOT

Well, I'll be split in two!

FIRST MAN

What you think of it, Flatfoot?

FLATFOOT

I must say! Look like a house wit' a warpin' cellar.

NOAH

Dis yere vessel is a boat.

FLATFOOT

When I was a little boy dey used to build boats down near de ribber, where de water was.

[*The others laugh.*]

NOAH

Dis time it's been arranged to have de water come up to de boat. [JAPHETH *looks belligerently over the rail of the Ark at* FLATFOOT. *To* JAPHETH.] Keep yo' shirt on, son.

SECOND WOMAN

[*To* THIRD WOMAN.] Now, you see de whole fam'ly's crazy.

THIRD WOMAN

Listen, dey ain't gonter 'taminate me. It was me dat started resolvin' dem both out o' de buryin' society.

ZEBA

When all dis water due up yere, Noah?

NOAH

You won't know when it gits yere, daughter.

ZEBA

Is she goin' to be a side-wheeler, like de Bessy-Belle?

FLATFOOT

No! If she was a side-wheeler she'd get her wheels all clogged wid sharks. She gonter have jus' one great big stern wheel, like de Commodore. Den if dey ain't 'nuf water why de big wheel kin stir some up.

[*General laughter. Two or three of the* GAMBLERS *enter and join the group, followed by* CAIN THE SIXTH.]

CAIN THE SIXTH

Dere's de fool an' his monument, jest like I said!

[*The* GAMBLERS *and* CAIN THE SIXTH *roar with laughter, slap their legs, etc., the members of the main group talk sotto voce to each other as* CAIN THE SIXTH *catches* ZEBA'S *eye.* FLATFOOT *is on her right and is not aware of* CAIN *the* SIXTH'S *presence.*]

NOAH

See how dey makin' out inside, son. [*Stops hammering.*]

[JAPHETH *exits into Ark.*]

[NOAH *turns and gazes towards the east.*]

CAIN THE SIXTH

Hello, honey.

ZEBA

[*Frightened but smiling.*]

Hello, sugah.

[77]

CAIN THE SIXTH

[*Pleasantly.*] Ain' dat my ol' frien' Flatfoot wid you?

ZEBA

Why, so 'tis! [FLATFOOT *is now listening.*] [*To* FLATFOOT.] He's got a gun.

CAIN THE SIXTH

No, I ain't.
   [*He lifts his hands over his head.* ZEBA *quickly advances and runs her hands lightly over his pockets.*]

ZEBA

[*Relieved.*] I guess he ain't.

CAIN THE SIXTH

No, I ain't got no gun for my ol' friend, Flatfoot.
[*He walks up to him.*]

FLATFOOT

[*Smiling.*] Hi, Cain. How's de boy?
   [CAIN *quickly presses his chest against* FLATFOOT'S, *his downstage arm sweeps around* FLATFOOT'S *body and his hand goes up to the small of* FLAT-FOOT'S *back.*]

CAIN THE SIXTH

[*Quietly, but triumphantly.*] I got a little *knife* fo' him.

[FLATFOOT *falls dead.*]

[*The laughter of the others stops and they look at the scene.* ZEBA *for a moment is terrified, her clenched hand pressed to her mouth. She looks at* CAIN THE SIXTH, *who is smiling at her. He tosses the knife on the ground and holds his hands out to her. She goes to him, smiling.*]

ZEBA

You sho' take keer of me, honey.

CAIN THE SIXTH

Dat's caize I think yo' wo'th takin' keer of. [*To the others.*] It's all right, folks. I jest had to do a little cleanin' up.

FIRST WOMAN

[*Smiling.*] You is de quickes' scoundrel.

FIRST GAMBLER

It was a nice quick killin'. Who was he?

SECOND WOMAN

[*Casually.*] Dey called him Flatfoot. From over de river. He wa'nt any good. He owed me for washin' for over a year.

THIRD WOMAN

Used to peddle muggles. Said it had a kick like reg'lar snow. Wasn't no good.

SECOND GAMBLER

Think we ought to bury him?

FIRST MAN

No, just leave him dere. Nobody comes up yere, 'cept ol' Manatee.
[*Indicates* NOAH. *Cries of "Ol' Manatee! Ol' Manatee, dat's good!"*]

NOAH

[*Still looking off.*] You bettah pray, you po' chillun. [*They all laugh.*]

FIRST WOMAN

We bettah pray? You bettah pray, Ol' Manatee?

ZEBA

You bettah pray for rain. [*Laughter again.*]

NOAH

Dat's what I ain't doin', sinners. Shem! Japheth! [*To others, as he points off. Patter of rain.*] Listen!

CAIN THE SIXTH

[*Casually.*] Doggone, I believe it *is* gonter shower a little.

FIRST GAMBLER

It do looks like rain.

FIRST WOMAN

I think I'll git on home. I got a new dress on.

ZEBA

Me, too. I wants to keep lookin' nice fo' my sweet papa.

[*She pats* CAIN THE SIXTH's *cheek.* CAIN THE SIXTH *hugs her.*]

NOAH

[*Almost frantically.*] Ham! Is de animals dere?

HAM

[*Off stage.*] Yes, sir, dere yere. We're comin'.

NOAH

Den bring 'em on.

[SHEM *and* JAPHETH *come on deck with their hammers. The stage begins to darken.*]

THIRD WOMAN

I guess we all might go home 'til de shower's over. Come on, papa.

SECOND GAMBLER

See you after supper, Noah. [*Crowd starts moving off* R.]

NOAH

God's gittin' ready to start, my sons. Let's git dis plankin' done.

[81]

ZEBA

Put a bix Texas on it, Noah, an' we'll use it fo' excursions.

[*There is a distant roll of thunder, there are cries of "Good night, Admiral." "See you later." "So long, Manatee," as the crowd goes off. The thunder rumbles again. There is the sound of increasing rain. The hammers of* SHEM *and* JAPHETH *sound louder and are joined by the sounds of other hammerers. There is a flash of lightning. The* CHOIR *begins "Dey Ol' Ark's a-Movering," the sounds on the Ark become faster and louder. The rush of rain grows heavier.*]

NOAH

Hurry! Hurry! Where are you, Ham?

HAM

[*Just off stage.*] Yere, I am, father, wid de animals.

NOAH

God's give us his sign. Send 'em up de gangplank.
[*An inclined plane is thrown against the Ark from the side of the stage by* HAM, *who cracks a whip.*]

HAM

Get on, dere.
[*The heads of two elephants are seen.*]

NOAH

Bring 'em on board! De Lawd is strikin' down de worl'!

[*The singing and the noises reach fortissimo as* HAM *cracks his whip again, and the rain falls on the stage.*]

[*The stage is darkened. The* CHOIR *continues singing in the darkness.*]

SCENE X

When the lights go up on scene, the Ark is at sea. Stationary waves run in front of it. The hillside has disappeared. The Ark is in the only lighted area.

SHEM *is smoking a pipe on the deck, leaning on the rail. A steamboat whistle blows three short and one long blast.* SHEM *is surprised. In a moment* HAM *appears, also with a pipe, and joins* SHEM *at the rail.*

SHEM

Who'd you think you was signallin'?

HAM

Dat wasn't me, dat was daddy.

SHEM

He think he gonter git a reply?

HAM

I don' know. He's been gittin' a heap of comfort out of dat likker.

SHEM

De kag's nearly empty, ain't it?

HAM

Pretty nearly almos'. [*They look over the rail. A pause.*] Seen anythin'?

SHEM

Dis mornin' I seen somethin' over dere migh'a' been a fish.

HAM

Dat's de big news of de week.

SHEM

How long you think dis trip's gonter las'?

HAM

I don' know! Rain fo'ty days 'n' fo'ty nights an' when dat stop' I thought sho' we'd come up ag'inst a san' bar o' somethin'. Looks now like all dat rain was jest a little incident of de trip. [*The whistle blows again.*] Doggone! I wish he wouldn't do dat. Fust thing we know he'll wake up dem animals ag'in.

[JAPHETH *appears.*]

SHEM

What de matter wit' de ol' man, Jape?

JAPHETH

Doggone, he say he had a dream dat we're nearly dere. Dat's why he pullin de whistle cord. See kin he git a' answer. [*He looks over the rail.*] Look to me like de same ol' territory.

[MRS. NOAH *appears on deck.*]

NOAH'S WIFE

You boys go stop yo' paw pullin' dat cord. He so full of likker he think he's in a race.

JAPHETH

He claim he know what he's doin'.

NOAH'S WIFE

I claim he gittin' to be a perfec' nuisance. Me an' yo' wives cain't hardly heah ou'sel'es think. [NOAH *appears, his hat rakishly tilted on his head. He goes to the railing and looks out.*] You 'spectin' company?

NOAH

Leave me be, woman. De watah don' look so rough today. De ol' boat's ridin' easier.

NOAH'S WIFE

Ridin' like a ol' mule!

NOAH

Yes, suh, de air don't feel so wet. Shem! 'Spose you sen' out 'nother dove. [SHEM *goes into the Ark.*] Ham, go git de soundin' line. Jape, keep yo' eye on de East.
[JAPHETH *goes to the end of the boat.*]

NOAH'S WIFE

As fo' you, I s'pose you'll help things along by takin' a little drink.

NOAH

Look yere, who's de pilot of dis vessel?

NOAH'S WIFE

Ol' Mister Dumb Luck.

NOAH

Well, see dat's where you don' know anythin'.

NOAH'S WIFE

I s'pose you ain't drunk as a fool?

NOAH

[*Cordially.*] I feel congenial.

NOAH'S WIFE

An' you look it. You look jest wonderful. I wonder if you'd feel so congenial if de Lawd was to show up?

NOAH

De Lawd knows what I'm doin', don' you worry 'bout dat.

NOAH'S WIFE

I wouldn't say anythin' ag'inst de Lawd. He suttinly let us know dey'd be a change in de weather. But I bet even de Lawd wonders sometimes why he ever put you in charge.

NOAH

Well, you let de Lawd worry' bout dat.
[SHEM *appears with the dove.*]

SHEM

Will I leave her go, Paw?

NOAH

Leave 'er go.
[*There is a chorus of "Good Luck, Dove," from the group as the dove flies off stage.* HAM *appears with the sounding line.*]
Throw 'er over, Boy.
[HAM *proceeds to do so.*]

NOAH'S WIFE

An' another thing——

HAM

Hey!

NOAH

[*Rushing to his side.*] What is it?

HAM

Only 'bout a inch! [*They lean over.*]

JAPHETH

It's gettin' light in de East.

[*As* HAM *works the cord up and down,* NOAH *and* NOAH'S WIFE *turn toward* JAPHETH. *The* CHOIR *begins "My Soul Is a Witness for the Lord."*]

NOAH

Praise de Lawd, so it is.

NOAH'S WIFE

Oh, dat's pretty.

NOAH

[*To* HAM.] An' de boat's stopped. We've landed. Shem, go down n' drag de fires an' dreen de boiler. Yo go help 'im, Ham.

JAPHETH

Look, Paw.

[*The dove wings back to the Ark with an olive branch in its mouth.*]

NOAH

’N’ yere’s de little dove wid greenery in its mouth! Take ’er down, Jape, so she kin tell de animals. [JAPHETH *exits after* SHEM *and* HAM *carrying the dove. To* MRS. NOAH.] Now, maybe you feel little different.

NOAH’S WIFE

[*Contritely.*] It was jes’ gittin’ to be so tiresome. I’m sorry, Noah.

NOAH

Dat’s all right, ol’ woman. [NOAH’S WIFE *exits.* NOAH *looks about him. The lights have changed and the water piece is gone and the ark is again on the hillside. Two mountains can be seen in the distance and a rainbow slowly appears over the Ark. The singing has grown louder.*] Thank you, Lawd, thank you very much indeed. Amen.

   [*The singing stops with the "Amen."* GOD *appears on the deck.*]

GOD

Yo’ welcome, Noah.
   [NOAH *turns and sees him.*]

NOAH

O, Lawd, it’s wonderful.

GOD

[*Looking about him.*] I sort of like it. I like de way you handled de ship, too, Noah.

NOAH

Was you watchin', Lawd?

GOD

Every minute. [*He smiles.*] Didn't de ol' lady light into you?

NOAH

[*Apologetically.*] She was kinda restless.

GOD

That's all right. I ain't blamin' nobody. I don' even min' you' cussin' an drinkin'. I figure a steamboat cap'n on a long trip like you had has a right to a little redeye, jest so he don' go crazy.

NOAH

Thank you, Lawd. What's de orders now?

GOD

All de animals safe?

NOAH

Dey all fin'n' dandy, Lawd.

GOD

Den I want you to open dat starboard door, an' leave 'em all out. Let 'em go down de hill. Den you an' de family take all de seeds 'n de sprouts an' begin plantin' ag'in. I'm startin' all over, Noah.

[NOAH *exits.* GOD *looks around.*]

GOD

Well, now we'll see what happens. [GOD *listens with a smile, as noises accompanying the debarking of the animals are heard. There are the cracks of whips, the voices of the men on the Ark, shouting: "Git along dere." "Whoa, take it easy." "Duck yo' head." "Keep in line dere,"* etc. *Over the Ark there is a burst of centrifugal shadows, and the sound of a myriad of wings.* GOD *smiles at the shadows.*] Dat's right, birds, fin' yo' new homes. [*Bird twitters are heard again.* GOD *listens a moment and rests an arm on the railing. He speaks softly.*] Gabriel, kin you spare a minute?"

[GABRIEL *appears.*]

GABRIEL

Yes, Lawd?

[*The sounds from the other side of the Ark are by now almost hushed. The* LORD *indicates the new world with a wave of the hand.*]

GOD

Well, it's did.

GABRIEL

[*Respectfully, but with no enthusiasm.*] So I take notice.

GOD

Yes, suh, startin' all over again.

GABRIEL

So I see.

GOD

[*Looking at him suddenly.*] Don' seem to set you up much.

GABRIEL

Well, Lawd, you see— [*He hesitates.*] 'Tain't none of my business.

GOD

What?

GABRIEL

I say, I don' know very much about it.

GOD

I know you don'. I jest wanted you to see it. [*A thought strikes him.*] Co'se, it ain' yo' business, Gabe. It's my business. 'Twas my idea. De whole thing was my idea. An' every bit of it's my business 'n nobody else's. De whole thing rests on my shoulders. I declare, I guess *dat's* why I feel so solemn an' serious, at dis particklar time. You know *dis* thing's turned into quite a proposition.

GABRIEL

·[*Tenderly*.] But, it's all right, Lawd, as you say, it's did.

GOD

Yes, suh, it's did. [*Sighs deeply. Looks slowly to the right and the left. Then softly*.] I only hope it's goin' to work out all right.

CURTAIN

THE GREEN PASTURES

PART TWO

PART TWO

Scene I

God's Office again.
Somewhere the Choir *is singing: "A City Called Heaven." In the office are* Two Women Cleaners. *One is scrubbing the floor, the other dusting the furniture. The one dusting stops and looks out the window. There is a whirr and a distant faint Boom. The* Choir *stops.*

FIRST CLEANER

Dat was a long way off.

SECOND CLEANER

[*At window.*] Yes, ma'am. An' dat must a' been a big one. Doggone, de Lawd mus' be mad fo' sho', dis mo'nin'. Dat's de fo'ty-six' thunde'-bolt since breakfast.

FIRST CLEANER

I wonder where at He's pitchin' dem.

SECOND CLEANER

My goodness, don' you know?

[97]

FIRST CLEANER

[*A little hurt.*] Did I know I wouldn't ask de question.

SECOND CLEANER

Every one of dem's bound fo' de earth.

FIRST CLEANER

De earth? You mean dat little ol' dreenin' place?

SECOND CLEANER

Dat's de planet. [*Another faint whirr and boom.*] Dere goes another.

FIRST CLEANER

Well, bless me. *I* didn't know dey was thunde'bolts.

SECOND CLEANER

Wha'd you think dey was?

FIRST CLEANER

[*Above desk.*] I wasn't sho', but I thought maybe He might be whittlin' a new star o' two, an' de noise was jest de chips fallin'.

SECOND CLEANER

Carrie, where you been? Don' you know de earth is de new scandal? Ever'body's talkin' 'bout it.

[98]

FIRST CLEANER

Dey kep' it from me.

SECOND CLEANER

Ain't you noticed de Lawd's been unhappy lately?

FIRST CLEANER

[*Thoughtfully.*] Yeah, He ain't been his old self.

SECOND CLEANER

What did you think was de matteh? Lumbago?

FIRST CLEANER

[*Petulantly.*] I didn't know. I didn't think it was fo' me t'inquieh.

SECOND CLEANER

Well, it jest so happens dat de Lawd is riled as kin be by dat measly little earth. Or I should say de scum dat's on it.

FIRST CLEANER

Dat's mankind down dere.

SECOND CLEANER

Dey mus' be scum, too, to git de Lawd so wukked up.

FIRST CLEANER

I s'pose so. [*Another whirr and boom.*] Looks like He's lettin' dem feel de wrath. Ain' dat a shame to plague de Lawd dat way?

SECOND CLEANER

From what I hear dey been beggin' fo' what dey're gittin'. My brother flew down to bring up a saint de other day and he say from what he see mos' of de population down dere has made de debbil king an' dey wukkin' in three shifts fo' him.

FIRST CLEANER

You cain't blame de Lawd.

SECOND CLEANER

Co'se you cain't. Dem human bein's 'd make any-body bile oveh. Ev'rytime de Lawd try to do sompin' fo' dem, doggone if dey don't staht some new ruckus.

FIRST CLEANER

I take notice He's been wukkin' in yere mo' dan usual.

SECOND CLEANER

I wish He'd let us ladies fix it up. Wouldn't take a minute to make dis desk gold-plated.

FIRST CLEANER

I 'spose He likes it dis way. De Lawd's kind o' ol' fashioned in some ways. I s'pose He keeps dis office plain an' simple on purpose.

SECOND CLEANER

[*Finishing her work.*] I don' see why.

FIRST CLEANER

[*Looking off.*] Well, it's kind of a nice place to come
to when He's studyin' somethin' impo'tant. 'Most evah-
thin' else in heaven's so fin' 'n' gran', maybe ev'ry now
an den He jest gits sick an' tired of de glory. [*She is
also collecting her utensils.*]

SECOND CLEANER

Maybe so. Jest de same I'd like to have a free hand
wid dis place for a while, so's I could gold it up.
[GOD *appears in the doorway.*]

GOD

Good mo'nin', daughters.

FIRST AND SECOND CLEANERS

Good mo'nin', Lawd. We was jest finishin'.

GOD

Go ahead den, daughters. [*Goes to the window.*]

FIRST AND SECOND CLEANERS

Yes, Lawd. [*They exeunt. Off stage.*] Good mo'nin',
Gabriel.
[*Off stage* GABRIEL *says, "Good mo'nin', sisters,"
and enters immediately. He stands in the door-*

way for a moment watching GOD—*a notebook
and pencil in his hand.*]

GOD

What's de total?

GABRIEL

[*Consulting the book.*] Eighteen thousand nine hun-
d'ed an' sixty for de mo'nin'. Dat's includin' de village
wid de fo'tune tellers. Dey certainly kin breed fast.

GOD

[*Solemnly.*] Dey displease me. Dey displease me
greatly.

GABRIEL

Want some more bolts, Lawd?

GOD

[*Looking through window.*] Look at 'em dere.
Squirmin' an fightin' an' bearin' false witness. Listen
to dat liar, dere. He don' intend to marry dat little gal.
He don' even love her. What did you say?

GABRIEL

Should I git mo' bolts?

GOD

Wait a minute. [*He carefully points his finger down
through the window.*] I'm goin' to git dat wicked man

myself. [*From a great distance comes an agonized cry: "Oh, Lawd!"* GOD *turns from the window.*] No use gittin' mo' thunde'bolts. Dey don' do de trick. [*He goes to the swivel chair and sits.*] It's got to be somethin' else.

GABRIEL

How would it be if you was to doom 'em all ag'in, like dat time you sent down de flood? I bet dat would make dem mind.

GOD

You see how much good de flood did. Dere dey is, jest as bad as ever.

GABRIEL

How about cleanin' up de whole mess of 'em and sta'tin' all over ag'in wid some new kind of animal?

GOD

An' admit I'm licked?

GABRIEL

[*Ashamedly.*] No, of co'se not, Lawd.

GOD

No, suh. No, suh. Man is a kind of pet of mine and it ain't right fo' me to give up tryin' to do somethin' wid him. Doggone, mankin' *mus'* be all right at de core or else why did I ever bother wid him in de first place? [*Sits at desk.*]

GABRIEL

It's jest dat I hates to see you worryin' about it, Lawd.

GOD

Gabe, dere ain't anythin' worth while anywheres dat didn't 'cause somebody some worryin'. I ain't never tol' you de trouble I had gittin' things started up yere. Dat's a story in itself. No, suh, de more I keep on bein' de Lawd de more I know I got to keep improvin' things. An' dat takes time and worry. De main trouble wid mankin' is he takes up so much of my time. He ought to be able to help hisself a little. [*He stops suddenly and cogitates.*] Hey, dere! I think I got it!

GABRIEL

[*Eagerly.*] What's de news?

GOD

[*Still cogitating.*] Yes, suh, dat seems like an awful good idea.

GABRIEL

Tell me, Lawd.

GOD

Gabriel, have you noticed dat every now an' den, mankin' turns out some pretty good specimens?

[104]

GABRIEL

Dat's de truth.

GOD

Yes, suh. Dey's ol' Abraham and Isaac an' Jacob an' all dat family.

GABRIEL

Dat's so, Lawd.

GOD

An' everyone of dem boys was a hard wukker an' a good citizen. We got to admit dat.

GABRIEL

Dey wouldn't be up yere flyin' wid us if dey hadn't been.

GOD

No, suh. An' I don' know but what de answer to de whole trouble is right dere.

GABRIEL

How you mean, Lawd?

GOD

Why, doggone it, de good man is de man dat keeps busy. I mean I been goin' along on de principle dat he was something like you angels—dat you ought to be able to give him somethin' an' den jest let him sit back an' enjoy it. Dat ain't so. Now dat I recollec' I put de first one down dere to take keer o' dat garden an' den I let him go ahead an' do nothin' but git into mischief. [*He rises.*] Sure, *dat's* it. He ain't *built* jest to fool 'roun' an' not do nothin'. Gabe, I'm gonter try a new scheme.

GABRIEL

[*Eagerly.*] What's de scheme, Lawd?

GOD

I'll tell you later. Send in Abraham, Isaac an' Jacob. [*A voice outside calls: "Right away, Lawd."*] You go tell dem to put dem bolts back in de boxes. I ain' gonter use dem ag'in a while.

GABRIEL

O. K., Lawd.

GOD

Was you goin' anywhere near de Big Pit?

GABRIEL

I could go.

GOD

Lean over de brink and tell Satan he's jest a plain fool if he thinks he kin beat anybody as big as me.

GABRIEL

Yes, suh, Lawd. Den I'll spit right in his eye. [GABRIEL *exits.*]

   [GOD *looks down through the window again to the earth below.*]

GOD

Dat new polish on de sun makes it powerful hot. [*He "r'ar back."*] Let it be jest a little bit cooler. [*He feels the air.*] Dat's nice. [*Goes to His desk. A knock on the door.*] Come in.

> [ABRAHAM, ISAAC *and* JACOB *enter. All are very old men, but the beard of* ABRAHAM *is the longest and whitest, and they suggest their three generations. They have wings that are not quite so big as those of the native angels.*]

ISAAC

Sorry we so long comin', Lawd. But Pappy and me had to take de boy [*Pointing to* JACOB] over to git him a can of wing ointment.

GOD

What was de matter, son?

JACOB

Dey was chafin' me a little. Dey fine now, thank you, Lawd.

GOD

Dat's good. Sit down an' make yo'selves comf'table. [*The three sit.* MEN: *"Thank you, Lawd."*] Men, I'm goin' to talk about a little scheme I got. It's one dat's goin' to affec' yo' fam'lies an' dat's why I 'cided I'd talk it over wid you, 'fo' it goes into ee-fect. I don' know whether you boys know it or not, but you is about de

[107]

three best men of one fam'ly dat's come up yere since I made little apples. Now I tell you what I'm gonter do. Seein' dat you human bein's cain't 'preciate anythin' lessen you fust wukk to git it and den keep strugglin' to hold it, why I'm gonter turn over a very valuable piece of property to yo' fam'ly, and den see what kin dey do with it. De rest of de worl' kin go jump in de river fo' all I keer. I'm gonter be lookin' out fo' yo' descendents only. Now den, seein' dat you boys know de country pretty tho'ly, where at does you think is de choice piece of property in de whole worl'? Think it over for a minute. I'm gonter let you make de s'lection.

ABRAHAM

If you was to ask me, Lawd, I don't think dey come any better dan de Land of Canaan.

GOD

[*To* ISAAC *and* JACOB.] What's yo' feelin' in de matter?

JACOB

[*After a nod from* ISAAC.] Pappy an' me think do we get a pick, dat would be it.

GOD

[*Goes to window again; looks out.*] De Land of Canaan. Yes, I guess dat's a likely neighborhood. It's all run over wid Philistines and things right now, but we kin clean dat up. [*He turns from the window and resumes his seat.*] All right. Now who do you boys think is de best of yo' men to put in charge down dere? You see I ain't been payin' much attention to anybody in partic'lar lately.

ISAAC

Does you want de brainiest or de holiest, Lawd? [MEN *look up.*]

GOD

I want de holiest. I'll make him brainy. [MEN appreciate the miracle.]

ISAAC

[*As* ABRAHAM *and* ISAAC *nod to him.*] Well, if you want A Number One, goodness, Lawd, I don't know where you'll git more satisfaction dan in a great-great-great-great grandson of mine.

GOD

Where's he at?

ISAAC

At de moment I b'lieve he's in de sheep business over in Midian County. He got in a little trouble down in Egypt, but t'wan't his doin'. He killed a man dat was abusin' one of our boys in de brick works. Of co'se you know old King Pharaoh's got all our people in bondage.

GOD

I heard of it. [*With some ire.*] Who did you think put them dere? [*The visitors lower their heads.*] It's all right, boys. [*All rise.*] I'm gonter take dem out of it. An' I'm gonter turn over de whole Land of Canaan to dem. An' do you know whose gonter lead dem dere? Yo' great, great, great, great grandson. Moses, ain't it?

ISAAC

Yes, Lawd.

GOD

[*Smiling.*] Yes. I been noticin' *him*.

ABRAHAM

It's quite a favor fo' de fam'ly, Lawd.

GOD

Dat's why I tol' you. You see, it so happens I love ·yo' fam'ly, an' I delight to honor it. Dat's all, gen'le-men. [*The three others rise and cross to the door, murmuring, "Yes, Lawd," "Thank you, Lawd," "Much obliged, Lawd." etc. The* CHOIR *begins, "My Lord's A-Writin' All De Time" pianissimo.* GOD *stands watching the men leave.*] Enjoy yo' selves. [*He goes to the window. The singing grows softer. He speaks through the window to the earth.*] I'm comin' down to see you, Moses, an' dis time my scheme's *got* to wukk.

[110]

[*The stage is darkened. The singing grows louder and continues until the lights go up on the next scene.*]

Scene II

The tableau curtains frame the opening of a cave, which is dimly lighted. A large turkey-berry bush is somewhere near the foreground. Moses *is seated on the grass eating his lunch from a basket in his lap.* Zipporah, *his wife, stands watching him. He is about forty,* Zipporah *somewhat younger. They are dressed inconspicuously. Moses stutters slightly when he speaks. He looks up to see* Zipporah *smiling.*

MOSES

What you smilin' at, Zipporah?

ZIPPORAH

Caize you enjoyin' yo'self.

MOSES

You is a good wife, Zipporah.

ZIPPORAH

You is a good husband, Moses. [Moses *wipes his mouth with a handkerchief and begins putting into the basket the various implements of the meal which had been on the ground about him.*] Why you suppose it's so dark yere today? Dey's no rain in de air.

MOSES

Seems like it's jest aroun' dis cave. Yo' father's house is got de sun on it. [*He looks in another direction.*] Looks all clear down toward Egypt.

ZIPPORAH

Co'se it *would* be fine weather in Egypt. De sky looks all right. Maybe it's gonter rain jest right yere. Why don't you move de sheep over to de other pasture?

MOSES

[*A bit puzzled.*] I don' know. It got dark like dis befo' you come along wid de dinner an' I was gonter stop you on de top of de hill. Den somethin' kep' me yere.

ZIPPORAH

S'pose it could be de Lawd warnin' you dat dey's 'Gyptians hangin' 'roun'?

MOSES

Dey may have fo'gotten all about dat killin' by now. Dey got a new Pharaoh down dere.

ZIPPORAH

An' I hear he's jest as mean to yo' people as his pappy was. I wouldn't put it pas' him to send soljahs all the way up yere fo' you.

MOSES

Dat's all right. De Lawd's looked after me so far, I don't 'spect him to fall down on me now. You better be gittin' home.

ZIPPORAH

[*Taking the basket.*] I'll be worryin' about you.

MOSES

[*Kissing her and then smiling.*] 'Parently de Lawd ain't. He knows I'm safe as kin be. Lemme see you feel dat way.

ZIPPORAH

You is a good man, Moses.

MOSES

I's a lucky man. [ZIPPORAH *exits with the basket.* MOSES *looks up at the sky.*] Dat's funny. De sun seems to be shinin' everyplace but right yere. It's shinin' on de sheep. Why ain't dey no cloud dere?

GOD

[*Off stage.*] Caize I want it to be like dat, Moses.

MOSES

[*Looking about him.*] Who's dat?

GOD

[*Off stage again.*] I'm de Lawd, Moses.

[113]

MOSES

[*Smiling.*] Dat's what you say. Dis yere shadow may be de Lawd's wukk, but dat voice soun' pretty much to me like my ol' brother Aaron.

GOD

[*Off stage.*] Den keep yo' eyes open, son. [*The turkey-berry bush begins to glow and then turns completely red.* MOSES *looks at it fascinated.*] Maybe you notice de bush ain't burnin' up.

MOSES

Dat's de truth.
   [MOSES *is full of awe but not frightened.*]

GOD

[*Off stage.*] Now you believe me?

MOSES

Co'se I does. It's wonderful.
   [*The light in the bush dies and* GOD *appears from behind it.*]

GOD

No, it ain't, Moses. It was jest a trick.

MOSES

'Scuse me doubtin' you, Lawd. I always had de feelin' you wuz takin' keer of me, but I never 'spected you'd fin' de time to talk wid me pussunly. [*He laughs.*] Dat was a good trick, Lawd. I'se seen some good ones, but dat was de beatenest.

GOD

Yo' gonter see lots bigger tricks dan dat, Moses. In fac', yo' gonter perfo'm dem.

MOSES

[*Incredulously.*] Me? I'm gonter be a tricker?

GOD

Yes, suh.

MOSES

An' do magic? Lawd, my mouth ain't got de quick talk to go wid it.

GOD

It'll come to you now.
            MOSES [*Now cured of stuttering*]
Is I goin' wid a circus?

GOD

[*Slowly and solemnly.*] Yo' is goin' down into Egypt, Moses, and lead my people out of bondage. To do dat I'm gonter make you de bes' tricker in de worl'.

MOSES

[*A little frightened.*] Egypt! You know I killed a man dere, Lawd. Won't dey kill me?

GOD

Not when dey see yo' tricks. You ain't skeered, is you?

MOSES

[*Simply and bravely.*] No, suh, Lawd.

GOD

Den yere's what I'm gonter do. Yo' people is my chillun, Moses. I'm sick and tired o' de way ol' King Pharaoh is treatin' dem, so I'se gonter take dem away, and yo' gonter lead dem. You gonter lead 'em out of Egypt an' across de river Jordan. It's gonter take a long time, and you ain't goin' on no excursion train. Yo' gonter wukk awful hard for somethin' yo' goin' to fin' when de trip's over.

MOSES

What's dat, Lawd?

GOD

It's de Land of Canaan. It's de bes' land I got. I've promised it to yo' people, an' I'm gonter give it to dem.

MOSES

Co'se, ol' King Pharaoh will do everything he kin to stop it.

GOD

Yes, an' dat's where de tricks come in. Dey tell me he's awful fond of tricks.

MOSES

I hear dat's *all* he's fon' of. Dey say if you can't take a rabbit out of a hat you cain't even git in to see him.

GOD

Wait'll you see de tricks you an' me's goin' to show him.

MOSES

[*Delightedly.*] Doggone! Huh, Lawd?

GOD

Yes, suh. Now de first trick—
[GOD *is lifting a stick which he carries.*]

MOSES

Jest a minute, Lawd. [GOD *halts the demonstration.*] I'm gonter learn de tricks and do just like you tell me, but I *know* it's gonter take me a little time to learn all dat quick talkin'. Cain't I have my brother Aaron go wid me? He's a good man.

GOD

I was gonter have him help you wid de Exodus. I guess he can watch, too.

MOSES

I'll call 'im. [*He turns as if to shout.*]

GOD

Wait. [MOSES *turns and looks at* GOD.] I'll *bring* him.
[*Softly*.] Aaron!

> [AARON *appears between* GOD *and* MOSES *in the*
> *mouth of the cave. He is a little taller than*
> MOSES *and slightly older. He, too, is dressed like*
> *a field hand.*]

AARON

[*Blankly*.] Hey!

> [MOSES *goes to him, takes his hand and leads him,*
> *bewildered, down to where* MOSES *had been*
> *standing alone.* AARON *then sees* GOD.]

MOSES

[*Almost in a whisper*.] It's all right.

GOD

Don't worry, son, I'm jest showin' some tricks.
Bringin' you yere was one of dem. [AARON *stares at*
GOD *as if hypnotized*.] Now den, you see dis yere rod?
Looks like a ordinary walking stick, don' it?

MOSES

Yes, Lawd.

GOD

Well, it ain't no ordinary walkin' stick, caize look.
[MOSES *leans forward*.] When I lays it down on de
groun'——

[*The stage is darkened. The* Choir *begins, "Go Down, Moses," and continues until the lights go up on the next scene.*]

SCENE III

The throne room of Pharaoh. *It suggests a Negro lodge room. The plain board walls are colored by several large parade banners of varying sizes, colors and materials, bordered with gold fringe and tassels on them. Some of the inscriptions on them read:*

SUBLIME ORDER OF PRINCES OF THE HOUSE OF PHARAOH
HOME CHAPTER

MYSTIC BROTHERS OF THE EGYPTIAN HOME GUARD
LADIES AUXILIARY, No. 1

SUPREME MAGICIANS AND WIZARDS OF THE UNIVERSE

PRIVATE FLAG OF HIS HONOR OLD KING PHARAOH

ROYAL YOUNG PEOPLE'S PLEASURE CLUB

ENCHANTED AND INVISIBLE CADETS OF EGYPT BOYS'
BRIGADE

[119]

There is one door up right and a window. The throne, an ordinary armchair with a drapery over its back, is on a dais. PHARAOH is seated on the throne. His crown and garments might be those worn by a high officer in a Negro lodge during a ritual. About the throne itself are high officials, several of them with plumed hats, clothing that suggests military uniforms, and rather elaborate sword belts, swords and scabbards. A few soldiers carrying spears are also in his neighborhood and one or two bearded ancients in brightly colored robes with the word "Wizard" on their conical hats. In the general group of men and women scattered elsewhere in the room Sunday finery is noticeable everywhere. Most of the civilians have bright "parade" ribbons and wear medals. In a cleared space immediately before the throne a CANDIDATE MAGICIAN is performing a sleight-of-hand trick with cards. PHARAOH watches him apathetically. He is receiving earnest attention from a few of the others, but the majority of the men and women are talking quietly among themselves. Beside the CANDIDATE MAGICIAN are several paraphernalia of previously demonstrated tricks.

CANDIDATE MAGICIAN

[*Holding up some cards.*] Now den, ol' King Pharaoh, watch dis. [*He completes a trick. There is a murmur of "Not Bad." "Pretty Good," etc. from a few of the watchers. PHARAOH makes no comment.*] Now, I

[120]

believe de cyard I ast you to keep sittin' on was de trey of diamonds, wasn't it?

PHARAOH

Yeah.

CANDIDATE MAGICIAN

Den kin I trouble you to take a look at it now? [PHARAOH *half rises to pick up a card he has been sitting on, and looks at it.*] I believe you'll now notice dat it's de King of Clubs? [PHARAOH *nods and shows the card to those nearest him. The* CANDIDATE MAGICIAN *waits for an audible approval and gets practically none.*] An' dat, ol' King Pharaoh, completes de puffohmance.

[*An elderly man in a uniform steps forward.*]

GENERAL

On behalf of my nephew I beg Yo' Honor to let him jine de ranks of de royal trickers and magicians.

PHARAOH

[*To the two* WIZARDS.] What do de committee think? [*The* WIZARDS *shake their heads.*] Dat's what I thought. He ain't good enough. I'd like to help you out, General, but you know a man's got to be a awful good tricker to git in de royal society dese days. You better go back an' steddy some mo', son. [*He lifts his voice and directs two soldiers guarding the door.*] Is de head magician reached de royal waitin' room yit?

[*One of the soldiers opens the door to look out.*] If he is, send him in.

> [*The soldier beckons to some one off stage, throws the door open, and announces to the court.*]

SOLDIER

De Head Magician of de land of Egypt.

> [*A very old and villainous man enters. His costume is covered with cabalistic and zodiacal signs. He advances to the King, the other magician and his uncle making way for him. He bows curtly to* PHARAOH.]

HEAD MAGICIAN

Good mo'nin', ol' King Pharaoh.

PHARAOH

Mo'nin', Professor. What's de news?

HEAD MAGICIAN

Evahthing's bein' carried out like you said.

PHARAOH

How's de killin' of de babies 'mongst de Hebrews comin' 'long?

HEAD MAGICIAN

Jes' like you ordered.

PHARAOH

[*Genially.*] Dey killed all of 'em, huh?

HEAD MAGICIAN

Do dey see one, dey kill 'im. You teachin' 'em a great lesson. Dey don' like it a-tall.

PHARAOH

[*Smiling.*] What do dey say?

HEAD MAGICIAN

[*Pawing the air inarticulately.*] I hates to tell in front of de ladies.

PHARAOH

Dey feels pretty bad, huh?

HEAD MAGICIAN

Dat's jest de beginnin' of it. Betwixt de poleece and de soljahs we killed about a thousan' of 'em las' night. Dat's purty good.

PHARAOH

[*Thoughtfully.*] Yeh, it's fair. I guess you boys is doin' all you kin. But I fin' I ain't satisfied, though.

HEAD MAGICIAN

How you mean, Yo' Honor?

PHARAOH

I mean I'd like to make dose Hebrew chillun realize dat I kin be even mo' of a pest. I mean I hates dem chillun. An' I'm gonter think of a way of makin' 'em even mo' mizzable.

HEAD MAGICIAN

But dey *ain't* anythin' meaner dan killin' de babies, King.

PHARAOH

Dey must be sump'n. Doggone, you is my head tricker, you put yo' brains on it. [*To the others.*] Quiet, whilst de Head Magician go into de silence.

HEAD MAGICIAN

[*After turning completely around twice, and a moment's cogitation.*] I tell you what I kin do. All de Hebrews dat ain't out to de buryin' grounds or in de hospitals is laborin' in de brick wukks.

PHARAOH

Yeh?

HEAD MAGICIAN

[*After a cackling laugh.*] How would it be to take de straw away from 'em and tell 'em dey's got to turn out jest as many bricks as usual? Ain't dat nasty?

PHARAOH

Purty triflin', but I s'pose it'll have to do for de time bein'. Where's de extreme inner guard? [*One of the military attendants comes forward.*] Go on out an' tell de sup'intendent to put dat into ee-ffect. [*The*

attendant bows and starts for the door. He stops as
Pharaoh *calls to him.*] Wait a minute! Tell 'im to chop
off de hands of anybody dat say he cain't make de
bricks dat way. [*The attendant salutes and exits, the
door being opened and closed by one of the soldiers.*]
Now what's de news in de magic line?

HEAD MAGICIAN

I ain't got very many novelties today, King, I bin
wukkin' too hard on de killin's. I'm so tired I don'
believe I could lift a wand.

[*There are murmurs of protest from the assemblage.*]

PHARAOH

Doggone, you was to 'a been de chief feature o' de
meetin' dis mawnin'. Look at de turn-out you got
account of me tellin' 'em you was comin'.

HEAD MAGICIAN

Well, dat's de way it is, King. Why don' you git de
wizards to do some spell castin'?

PHARAOH

Dey say it's in de cyards dat dey cain't wukk till high
noon. [*He glances at the* Wizards.] Think mebbe you
kin cheat a little?

FIRST WIZARD

Oh dat cain't be done, King.

PHARAOH

Well, we might as well adjourn, den. Looks to me like de whole program's shot to pieces. [*He starts to rise, when there is a furious banging on the door.*] What's de idea, dere? See who dat is. [*The soldiers open the door.* MOSES *and* AARON *enter, pushing the two soldiers aside and coming down in front of* PHARAOH. *The soldiers are bewildered and* PHARAOH *is angry.*] Say, who tol' you two baboons you could come in yere?

MOSES

Is you ol' King Pharaoh?

PHARAOH

Dat's me. Did you heah what I asked you?

MOSES

My name is Moses, and dis is my brother Aaron. [*Murmur of "Hebrews" spreads through the room.*]

PHARAOH

[*In a rage.*] Is you Hebrews?

MOSES

Yes, suh.

PHARAOH

[*Almost screaming.*] Put 'em to de sword!
  [*As the courtiers approach,* AARON *suddenly discloses the rod, which he swings once over his*

[126]

head. The courtiers draw back as if their hands had been stung. Cries of "Hey!" "Lookout," etc.]

MOSES

Keep outside dat circle.

[*The courtiers nearest* MOSES *and* AARON *look at each other, exclaiming ad lib., "Did you feel dat?" "What is dat?" "What's goin' on, heah?" "My hands is stingin'!" etc.*]

PHARAOH

[*Puzzled but threatening.*] What's de idea yere?

MOSES

We is magicians, ol' King Pharaoh.

PHARAOH

[*To the* HEAD MAGICIAN.] Put a spell on 'em. [*The* HEAD MAGICIAN *stands looking at them bewildered. To* MOSES.] I got some magicians, too. We'll see who's got de bes' magic. [MOSES *and* AARON *laugh. Most of the courtiers are cowering. To the* HEAD MAGICIAN.] Go ahead, give 'em gri-gri.

MOSES

Sure, go ahead.

PHARAOH

Hurry up, dey's laughin' at you. What's de matter?

HEAD MAGICIAN

I cain't think of de right spell.

PHARAOH

[*Now frightened himself.*] You mean dey got even *you* whupped?

HEAD MAGICIAN

Dey's got a new kind of magic.

PHARAOH

[*Gazes at* HEAD MAGICIAN *a moment, bewildered. To the* WIZARDS.] I s'pose if de Professor cain't, you cain't.

FIRST WIZARD

Dat's a new trick, King.

HEAD MAGICIAN

[*Rubbing his fingers along his palms.*] It's got 'lectricity in it!

PHARAOH

Hm, well dat may make it a little diff'rent. So you boys is magicians, too?

MOSES

Yes, suh.

PHARAOH

Well, we's always glad to see some new trickers in de co't, dat is if dey good. [*He glances about him.*] You look like you is O. K.

[128]

MOSES

Dat's what we claims, ol' King Pharaoh. We think we's de best in de worl'.

PHARAOH

You certainly kin talk big. Jest what is it you boys would like?

MOSES

We came to show you some tricks. Den we's goin' to ask you to do somethin' for us.

PHARAOH

Well, I s'pose you know I'm a fool for conjurin'. If a man kin show me some tricks I ain't seen, I goes out of my way to do him a favor.

MOSES

Dat's good. Want to see de first trick?

PHARAOH

It ain't goin' to hurt nobody?

MOSES

Dis one won't.

PHARAOH

Go ahead.

MOSES

Dis yere rod my brother has looks jes' like a walkin'
stick, don't it?

[*The courtiers now join the King in interest.*]

PHARAOH

Uh huh. Le's see.

[AARON *hands him the rod, which* PHARAOH *inspects and returns.*]

MOSES

Well, look what happens when he lays it on de
groun'.

[AARON *places the rod on the second step of the
throne. It turns into a lifelike snake. There are
exclamations from the assemblage.*]

PHARAOH

Dat's a good trick! Now turn it back into a walkin'
stick again. [AARON *picks it up and it is again a rod.
Exclamations of "Purty good!" "Dat's all right!"
"What do you think of that!" etc.*] Say, you is good
trickers!

MOSES

You ain't never seen de beat of us. Now I'm goin' to
ask de favor.

PHARAOH

Sure, what is it?

MOSES

[*Solemnly.*] Let de Hebrew chillun go!

PHARAOH

[*Rises and stares at them. There is a murmur of "Listen to 'im!" "He's got nerve!" "I never in my life!" "My goodness!" etc.*] What did you say?

MOSES

Let de Hebrew chillun go.
[PHARAOH *seats himself again.*]

PHARAOH

[*Slowly.*] Don' you know de Hebrews is my slaves?

MOSES

Yes, suh.

PHARAOH

Yes, suh, my slaves. [*There is a distant groaning.*] Listen, and you kin hear 'em bein' treated like slaves. [*He calls toward the window.*] What was dey doin' den?

MAN NEAR THE WINDOW

Dey's jest gettin' de news down in de brick-yard.

[131]

PHARAOH

I won't let them go. [*He snorts contemptuously.*]
Let's see another trick.

MOSES

Yes, suh, yere's a better one. [*He lowers his head.*]
Let's have a plague of de flies.

> [AARON *raises the rod. The room grows dark and
> a great buzzing of flies is heard. The courtiers
> break out in cries of "Get away fum me!" "Take
> 'em away!" "De place is filled with flies!" "Dis
> is terrible!" "Do sump'n, Pharaoh!"*]

PHARAOH

[*Topping the others.*] All right—stop de trick!

MOSES

Will you let de Hebrews go?

PHARAOH

Sho' I will. Go ahead stop it!

MOSES

[*Also above the others.*] Begone!

> [*The buzzing stops and the room is filled with
> light again, as* AARON *lowers the rod. All except*
> MOSES AND AARON *are brushing the flies from
> their persons.*]

PHARAOH

[*Laughing.*] Doggone, dat was a good trick! [*The others, seeing they are uninjured, join in the laughter, with exclamations of "Doggone!" "You all right?" "Sho' I'm all right." "Didn' hurt me," etc.*] You *is* good trickers.

MOSES

Will you let de Hebrew chillun go?

PHARAOH

[*Sitting down again.*] Well, I'll tell you, boys. I'll tell you sump'n you didn' know. You take me, *I'm* a pretty good tricker, an' I jest outtricked you. So, bein' de bes' tricker, I don' think I will let 'em go. You got any mo' tricks yo'self?

MOSES

Yes, suh. Dis is a little harder one. [AARON *lifts the rod.*] Gnats in de mill pon', gnats in de clover, gnats in de tater patch, stingin' all over.

> [*The stage grows dark again. There is the humming of gnats and the slapping of hands against faces and arms, and the same protests as were heard with the flies, but with more feeling, "I'm gittin' stung to death!" "I'm all stung!" "Dey're like hornets!" "Dey's on my face!" etc.*]

PHARAOH

Take 'em away, Moses!

[*His voice drowning the others.*] If I do, will you let 'em go?

Sho' I will, dis time.

Do you mean it?

Co'se I mean it! Doggone, one just stang me on de nose.

Begone! [*Lights come up as* AARON *lowers the rod. There is a moment of general recovery again.* PHARAOH *rubs his nose, looks at his hands, etc., as do the others.*] Now, how about it?

[*Smiling.*] Well, I'll tell you, Moses. Now dat de trick's over—

[MOSES *takes a step toward* PHARAOH.]

Listen, Pharaoh. You been lyin' to me, and I'm gittin' tired of it.

I ain't lyin', I'm trickin', too. You been trickin' me and I been trickin' you.

MOSES

I see. Well, I got one mo' trick up my sleeve which I didn't aim to wukk unless I had to. Caize when I does it, I cain't undo it.

PHARAOH

Wukk it an' I'll trick you right back. I don' say you ain't a good tricker, Moses. You is one of de best I ever seen. But I kin outtrick you. Dat's all.

MOSES

It ain't only me dat's goin' to wukk dis trick. It's me an' de Lawd.

PHARAOH

Who?

MOSES

De Lawd God of Israel.

PHARAOH

I kin outtrick you an' de Lawd too!

MOSES

[*Angrily.*] Now you done it, ol' King Pharaoh. You been mean to de Lawd's people, and de Lawd's been easy on you caize you didn' know no better. You been givin' me a lot of say-so-and no do-so, and I didn' min' dat. But now you've got to braggin' dat you's better dan de Lawd, and dat's too many.

[135]

PHARAOH

You talk like a preacher, an' I never did like to hear preachers talk.

MOSES

You ain't goin' to like it any better, when I strikes down de oldes' boy in every one of yo' people's houses.

PHARAOH

Now you've given up trickin' and is jest lyin'. [*He rises.*] Listen, I'm Pharaoh. I do de strikin' down yere. I strike down my enemies, and dere's no one in all Egypt kin kill who he wants to, 'ceptin' me.

MOSES

I'm sorry, Pharaoh. Will you let de Hebrews go?

PHARAOH

You heard my word. [AARON *is lifting his rod again at a signal from* MOSES.] Now, no more tricks or I'll—

MOSES

Oh, Lawd, you'll have to do it, I guess. Aaron, lift de rod.

[*There is a thunderclap, darkness and screams. The lights go up. Several of the younger men on the stage have fallen to the ground or are being held in the arms of the horrified elders.*]

PHARAOH

What have you done yere? Where's my boy?
  [*Through the door come four men bearing a
  young man's body.*]

FIRST OF THE FOUR MEN

King Pharaoh.
  [PHARAOH *drops into his chair, stunned, as the
  dead boy is brought to the throne.*]

PHARAOH

[*Grief-stricken.*] Oh, my son, my fine son.
  [*The courtiers look at him with mute appeal.*]

MOSES

I'm sorry, Pharaoh, but you cain't fight de Lawd.
Will you let his people go?

PHARAOH

Let them go.
  [*The lights go out. The* CHOIR *begins, "Mary
  Don't You Weep," and continues until it is
  broken by the strains of "I'm Noways Weary and
  I'm Noways Tired." The latter is sung by many
  more voices than the former, and the cacophony
  ends as the latter grows in volume and the lights
  go up on the next scene.*]

Scene IV

The Children of Israel *are marching on the tread-mill and now singing fortissimo. They are of all ages and most of them are ragged. The men have packs on their shoulders, one or two have hand carts. The line stretches across the stage. It is nearing twilight, and the faces of the assemblage are illumined by the rays of the late afternoon sun. The upper treadmill carries a gradu- ally rising and falling middle distance past the march- ers. The foot of a mountain appears; a trumpet call is heard as the foot of the mountain reaches stage center. The marchers halt. The picture now shows the moun- tain running up out of sight off right. The singing stops. A babel of "What's de matter?" "Why do we stop?" "Tain't sundown yet!" "What's happened?" "What's goin' on?" "What are they blowin' for?" etc. Those looking ahead begin to murmur. "It's Moses," "Moses." "What's happened to him?" The others take up the repetition of "Moses," and* Moses *enters, on the arm of* Aaron. *He is now an old man, as is his brother, and he totters toward the center of the stage. Cries of "What's de matter, Moses?" "You ain't hurt, is you?" "Ain't that too bad?" etc. He slowly seats himself on the rock at the foot of the mountain.*

AARON

How you feelin' now, brother?

MOSES

I'm so weary, Aaron. Seems like I was took all of a sudden.

AARON

Do we camp yere?

MOSES

[*Pathetically*.] No, you got to keep goin'.

AARON

But you cain't go no further tonight, brother.

MOSES

Dis never happened to me befo'.

A YOUNG WOMAN

But you's a ol' man, now, Father Moses. You cain't expect to go as fas' as we kin.

MOSES

But de Lawd said I'd do it. He said I was to show you de Promised Land. Fo'ty years, I bin leadin' you.

I led you out o' Egypt. I led you past Sinai, and through de wilderness. Oh, I cain't fall down on you now!

AARON

Le's res' yere fo' de night. Den we'll see how you feel in de mo'nin'.

MOSES

We tol' de scouts we'd meet 'em three miles furder on. I hate fo' 'em to come back all dis way to report. 'Tis gettin' a little dark, ain't it?

AARON

It ain't dark, Brother.

MOSES

No, it's my eyes.

AARON

Maybe it's de dust.

MOSES

No, I jest cain't seem to see. Oh, Lawd, dey cain't have a blind man leadin' 'em! Where is you, Aaron?

AARON

I'se right yere, Moses.

MOSES

Do you think— [*Pause.*] Oh! Do you think it's de time He said?

How you mean, Moses?

[*Crowd look from one to another in wonder.*]

MOSES

He said I could lead 'em to de Jordan, dat I'd *see* de Promised Land, and dat's all de further I could go, on account I broke de laws. Little while back I thought *I did* see a river ahead, and a pretty land on de other side. [*Distant shouts "Hooray!" "Yere dey are!" "Dey travelled quick." etc.*] Where's de young leader of de troops? Where's Joshua?

[*The call "Joshua" is taken up by those on the right of the stage, followed almost immediately by "Yere he is!" "Moses wants you!" etc.*]

[JOSHUA *enters. He is a fine looking Negro of about thirty.*]

JOSHUA

[*Going to* MOSES' *side.*] Yes, suh.

MOSES

What's de shoutin' 'bout, Joshua?

JOSHUA

De scouts is back wid de news. De Jordan is right ahead of us, and Jericho is jest on de other side. Moses, we're dere! [*There are cries of "Hallelujah!" "De Lawd*

*be praised!" "Hooray!" "De Kingdom's comin'!" etc.
With a considerable stir among the marchers, several
new arrivals crowd in from right, shouting "Moses,
we're dere!"* JOSHUA *seeing the newcomers.*] Yere's de
scouts!

> [*Three very ragged and dusty young men advance
> to* MOSES.]

MOSES

[*As the shouting dies.*] So it's de River Jordan?

FIRST SCOUT

Yes, suh.

MOSES

All we got to take is de city of Jericho.

FIRST SCOUT

Yes, suh.

MOSES

Joshua, you got to take charge of de fightin' men,
an' Aaron's gotta stay by de priests.

JOSHUA

What about you?

MOSES

You are leavin' me behind. Joshua, you gonter get
de fightin' men together and take dat city befo' sundown.

JOSHUA

It's a big city, Moses, wid walls all 'round it. We
ain't got enough men.

MOSES

You'll take it, Joshua.

JOSHUA

Yes, suh, but how?

MOSES

Move up to de walls wid our people. Tell de priests to go wid you with de rams' horns. You start marchin' 'roun' dem walls, and den—

JOSHUA

Yes, suh.

MOSES

De Lawd'll take charge, jest as he's took charge ev'y time I've led you against a city. He ain't never failed, has he?

SEVERAL VOICES

No, Moses. [*All raise their heads.*]

MOSES

And he ain't goin' to fail us now. [*He prays. All bow.*] Oh, Lawd, I'm turnin' over our brave young men to you, caize I know you don' want me to lead 'em any further. [*Rises.*] Jest like you said, I've got to de Jordan but I cain't git over it. An' yere dey goin' now to take de city of Jericho. In a little while dey'll be marchin' 'roun' it. An' would you please be so good as to tell 'em what to do? Amen. [*To* JOSHUA.] Go ahead. Ev'ybody follows Joshua now. Give de signal to move on wid e'vything. [*A trumpet is heard.*] You camp fo' de night in de City of Jericho. [Moses *seats himself on the rock.*]

JOSHUA

Cain't we help you, Moses?

MOSES

You go ahead. De Lawd's got his plans fo' me. Soun' de signal to march. [*Another trumpet call is heard. The company starts marching off.* Aaron *lingers a moment.*] Take care of de Ark of de Covenant, Aaron.

AARON

Yes, Brother. Good-bye.

MOSES

Good-bye, Aaron. [*The singing is resumed softly and dies away. The last of the marchers has disappeared.*] Yere I is, Lawd. De chillun is goin' into de Promised Land. [God *enters from behind the hill. He walks to* Moses, *puts his hands on his shoulders.*] You's with me, ain't you, Lawd?

GOD

Co'se I is.

MOSES

Guess I'm through, Lawd. Jest like you said I'd be, when I broke de tablets of de law. De ol' machine's broke down.

GOD

Jest what was it I said to you, Moses? Do you remember?

MOSES

You said I couldn't go into de Promised Land.

GOD

Dat's so. But dat ain't all dey was to it.

MOSES

How you mean, Lawd?

GOD

Moses, you been a good man. You been a good leader of my people. You got me angry once, dat's true. And when you anger me I'm a God of Wrath. But I never meant you wasn't gonter have what was comin' to you. An' I ain't goin' to do you out of it, Moses. It's jest de country acrost de River dat you ain't gonter enter. You gonter have a Promised Land. I been gettin' it ready fo' you, fo' a long time. Kin you stand up?

MOSES

[Rising, with GOD's help.] Yes, suh, Lawd.

GOD

Come on, I'm goin' to show it to you. We goin' up dis hill to see it. Moses, it's a million times nicer dan de Land of Canaan. [They start up the hill.]

MOSES

I cain't hardly see.

GOD

Don't worry. Dat's jest caize you so old.

[*They take a step or two up the hill, when* MOSES
stops suddenly.]

MOSES

Oh!

GOD

What's de matter?

MOSES

We cain't be doin' dis!

GOD

Co'se we kin!

MOSES

But I fo'got! I fo'got about Joshua and de fightin'
men!

GOD

How about 'em?

MOSES

Dey're marchin' on Jericho. I tol' 'em to march
aroun' de walls and den de Lawd would be dere to
tell 'em what to do.

GOD

Dat's all right. He's dere.

MOSES

Den who's dis helpin' me up de hill?

GOD

Yo' faith, yo' God.

MOSES

And is you over dere helpin' them too, Lawd? Is you goin' to tell dem poor chillun what to do?

GOD

Co'se I is. Listen, Moses. I'll show you how I'm helpin' dem.

> [*From the distance comes the blast of the rams' horns, the sound of crumbling walls, a roar, and a moment's silence. The* CHOIR *begins "Joshua Fit De Battle of Jericho" and continues through the rest of the scene.*]

MOSES

You did it, Lawd! You've tooken it! Listen to de chillun'—dey's in de Land of Canaan at last! You's de only God dey ever was, ain't you, Lawd?

GOD

[*Quietly.*] Come on, ol' man. [*They continue up the hill.*]

> [*The stage is darkened.*]

MR. DESHEE [*In the dark*]

But even dat scheme didn' work. Caize after dey got into the Land of Canaan dey went to de dogs again.

And dey went into bondage again. Only dis time it
was in de City of Babylon.

[*The* CHOIR, *which has been singing "Cain't Stay
Away," stops as the next scene begins.*]

SCENE V

*Under a low ceiling is a room vaguely resembling a
Negro night club in New Orleans. Two or three long
tables run across the room, and on the left is a table on
a dais with a gaudy canopy above it. The table bears
a card marked "Reserved for King and guests."*

*Flashy young men and women are seated at the
tables. About a dozen couples are dancing in the foreground to the tune of a jazz orchestra. The costumes
are what would be worn at a Negro masquerade to
represent the debauchees of Babylon.*

FIRST MAN

When did yuh git to Babylon?

SECOND MAN

I jes' got in yesterday.

THIRD MAN [*Dancing*]

How do you like dis baby, Joe?

FOURTH MAN

Hot damn! She could be de King's pet!

A WOMAN

Anybody seen my papa?

THIRD MAN

Don' fo'git de dance at de High Priest's house to-morrow.

[*The dance stops as a bugle call is heard. Enter* MASTER OF CEREMONIES.]

MASTER OF CEREMONIES

Stop! Tonight's guest of honor, de King of Babylon an' party of five.

[*Enter the* KING *and five girls. The* KING *has on an imitation ermine cloak over his conventional evening clothes and wears a diamond tiara. All rise as the* KING *enters, and sing, "Hail, de King of Bab—Bab—Babylon."*]

KING

Wait till you see de swell table I got. [*He crosses the stage to his table. The girls are jabbering.*] Remind me to send you a peck of rubies in de mo'nin'.

MASTER OF CEREMONIES

Ev'nin', King!

KING

Good ev'nin'. How's de party goin'?

MASTER OF CEREMONIES

Bes' one we ever had in Babylon, King.

KING

Any Jew boys yere?

MASTER OF CEREMONIES

[*Indicating some of the others.*] Lot o' dem yere.
I kin go git mo' if you want 'em.

KING

I was really referrin' to de High Priest. He's a 'ticlar
frien' o' mine an' he might drop in. You know what
he look like?

MASTER OF CEREMONIES

No, suh, but I'll be on de look-out fo' him.

KING

O.K. Now le's have a li'l good time.

MASTER OF CEREMONIES

Yes, suh. [*To the orchestra.*] Let 'er go, boys.
  [*The music begins, waiters appear with food and
  great urns painted gold and silver, from which
  they pour out wine for the guests. The* MASTER
  OF CEREMONIES *exits. The* KING'S *dancing-girls
  go to the middle of the floor, and start to dance.
  The* KING *puts his arms about the waists of two
  girls, and draws them to him.*]

KING

Hot damn! Da's de way! Let de Jew boys see our gals kin dance better'n dere's. [*There is an ad lib. babel of "Da's de truth, King!" "I don't know—we got some good gals, too!" etc.*] Dey ain' nobody in de worl' like de Babylon gals.

> [*The dancing grows faster, the watchers keep time with hand-claps. The door at the left opens suddenly, and the* PROPHET, *a patriarchal, ragged figure enters. He looks belligerently about the room, and is followed almost immediately by the* MASTER OF CEREMONIES.]

PROPHET

Stop! [*The music and the dancers halt.*]

KING

What's the idea, bustin' up my party?

MASTER OF CEREMONIES

He said he was expected, King. I thought mebbe he was de—

KING

Did you think he was de High Priest of de Hebrews? Why, he's jest an ol' bum! De High Priest is a fashion plate. T'row dis ole bum out o' yere!

PROPHET

Stop!

[*Those who have been advancing to seize him stop, somewhat amused.*]

KING

Wait a minute. Don't throw him out. Let's see what he has to say.

PROPHET

Listen to me, King of Babylon! I've been sent yere by de Lawd God Jehovah. Don't you dare lay a hand on de Prophet!

KING

Oh, you're a prophet, is yuh? Well, you know we don' keer much fo' prophets in dis part of de country.

PROPHET

Listen to me, sons and daughters of Babylon! Listen, you children of Israel dat's given yo'selves over to de evil ways of yo' oppressors! You're all wallowin' like hogs in sin, an' de wrath of Gawd ain' goin' to be held back much longer! I'm tellin' you, repent befo' it's too late. Repent befo' Jehovah casts down de same fire dat burned up Sodom and Gomorrah. Repent befo' de—

[*During this scene yells increase as the* PROPHET *continues.*]

[*The* HIGH PRIEST *enters Left. He is a fat volup-
tuary, elaborately clothed in brightly colored
robes. He walks in hand in hand with a gaudily
dressed "chippy."*]

HIGH PRIEST

[*Noise stops.*] Whoa, dere! What you botherin' the
King fo'?

PROPHET

[*Wheeling.*] And you, de High Priest of all Israel,
walkin' de town wid a dirty li'l tramp.

KING

Seems to be a frien' o' yours, Jake.

HIGH PRIEST

[*Crossing to the* KING *with his girl.*] Aw, he's one
of dem wild men, like Jeremiah and Isaiah. Don' let
him bother you none. [*Pushes* PROPHET *aside and goes
to* KING's *table.*]

PROPHET

You consort with harlots, an' yo' pollution in the
sight of de Lawd. De Lawd God's goin' to smite you
down, jest as he's goin' to smite down all dis wicked
world! [*Grabs* HIGH PRIEST *and turns him around.*]

KING

[*Angrily against the last part of the preceding
speech.*] Wait a minute. I'm getting tired of this. Don'

throw him out. Jest kill him! [*There is the sound of a shot. The* PROPHET *falls.*]

PROPHET

Smite 'em down, Lawd, like you said. Dey ain't a decent person left in de whole world.

[*He dies.* MASTER OF CEREMONIES, *revolver in hand, looks down at the* PROPHET.]

MASTER OF CEREMONIES

He's dead, King.

KING

Some of you boys take him out.

[*A couple of young men come from the background and walk off with the body.*]

HIGH PRIEST

Don' know whether you should'a done that, King.

KING

Why not?

HIGH PRIEST

I don' know whether de Lawd would like it.

KING

Now, listen, Jake. You know yo' Lawd ain't payin' much attention to dis man's town. Except fo' you boys, it's tho'ly protected by de Gods o' Babylon.

HIGH PRIEST

I know, but jest de same—

KING

Look yere, s'pose I give you a couple hund'ed pieces
of silver. Don' you s'pose you kin arrange to persuade
yo' Gawd to keep his hands off?

HIGH PRIEST

[*Oilily.*] Well of co'se we could try. I dunno how
well it would work.

　　[*As the* HIGH PRIEST *speaks, The* KING *claps his
　　hands.* MASTER OF CEREMONIES *enters with bag
　　of money.*]

KING

Yere it is.

HIGH PRIEST

[*Smiling.*] I guess we kin square things up. [*He
prays—whiningly.*] Oh Lawd, please forgive my po'
frien' de King o' Babylon. He didn't know what he
was doin' an'—

　　[*There is a clap of thunder, darkness for a second.
　　The lights go up and* GOD *is standing in the
　　center of the room.*]

GOD

[*In a voice of doom.*] Dat's about enough. [*The
guests are horrified.*] I's stood all I kin from you. I

tried to make dis a good earth. I helped Adam, I helped Noah, I helped Moses, an' I helped David. What's de grain dat grew out of de seed? Sin! Nothin' but sin throughout de whole world. I've given you ev'y chance. I sent you warriors and prophets. I've given you laws and commandments, an' you betrayed my trust. Ev'ything I've given you, you've defiled. Ev'y time I've fo'given you, you've mocked me. An' now de High Priest of Israel tries to trifle wid my name. Listen, you chillun of darkness, yo' Lawd is tried. I'm tired of de struggle to make you worthy of de breath I gave you. I put you in bondage ag'in to cure you an' yo' worse dan you was amongst de flesh pots of Egypt. So I renounce you. Listen to the words of yo' lawd God Jehovah, for dey is de last words yo' ever hear from me. I repent of dese people dat I have made and I will deliver dem no more.

[*There is darkness and cries of "Mercy!" "Have pity, Lawd!" "We didn' mean it, Lawd!" "Forgive us, Lawd!" etc. The* CHOIR *sings "Death's Gwinter Lay His Cold Icy Hands On Me" until the lights go up on the next scene.*]

SCENE VI

GOD *is writing at his desk. Outside, past the door, goes* HOSEA, *a dignified old man, with wings like* JACOB'S. GOD, *sensing his presence, looks up from the paper he is examining, and follows him out of the corner of his eye. Angrily he resumes his work as soon as* HOSEA *is out of sight. There is a knock on the door.*

GOD

Who is it?
[GABRIEL *enters.*]

GABRIEL

It's de delegation, Lawd.

GOD

[*Wearily.*] Tell 'em to come in.
[ABRAHAM, ISAAC, JACOB, *and* MOSES *enter.*]
Good mo'nin', gen'lemen.

THE VISITORS

Good mo'nin', Lawd.

GOD

What kin I do for you?

MOSES

You know, Lawd. Go back to our people.

GOD

[*Shaking his head.*] Ev'ry day fo' hund'ed's of years you boys have come in to ask dat same thing. De answer is still de same. I repented of de people I made.

I said I would deliver dem no more. Good mo'nin', gen'lemen. [*The four visitors rise and exeunt.* GABRIEL *remains.*] Gabe, why do dey do it?

GABRIEL

I 'spect dey think you gonter change yo' mind.

GOD

[*Sadly.*] Dey don' know me. [HOSEA *again passes the door. His shadow shows on wall.* GABRIEL *is perplexed, as he watches.* GOD *again looks surreptitiously over His shoulder at the passing figure.*] I don' like dat, either.

GABRIEL

What, Lawd?

GOD

Dat man.

GABRIEL

He's jest a prophet, Lawd. Dat's jest old Hosea. He jest come up the other day.

GOD

I know. He's one of de few dat's come up yere since I was on de earth last time.

GABRIEL

Ain' been annoyin' you, has he?

GOD

I don' like him walkin' past de door.

GABRIEL

All you got to do is tell him to stop, Lawd.

GOD

Yes, I know. I don' want to tell him. He's got a right up yere or he wouldn' be yere.

GABRIEL

You needn' be bothered by him hangin' aroun' de office all de time. I'll tell 'im. Who's he think he—

GOD

No, Gabe. I find it ain't in me to stop him. I sometimes jest wonder why he don' come in and say hello.

GABRIEL

You want him to do dat?
[*He moves as if to go to the door.*]

GOD

He never has spoke to me, and if he don' wanta come in, I ain't gonter make him. But dat ain't de worst of it, Gabriel.

GABRIEL

What is, Lawd?

[159]

GOD

Ev'y time he goes past de door I hears a voice.

GABRIEL

One of de angels?

GOD

[*Shaking his head.*] It's from de earth. It's a man.

GABRIEL

You mean he's prayin'?

GOD

No, he ain't exactly prayin'. He's jest talkin' in such a way dat I got to lissen. His name is Hezdrel.

GABRIEL

Is he on de books?

GOD

No, not yet. But ev'y time dat Hosea goes past I hear dat voice.

GABRIEL

Den tell *it* to stop.

GOD

I find I don' want to do that, either. Dey's gettin' ready to take Jerusalem down dere. Dat was my big fine city. Dis Hezdrel, he's jest one of de defenders. [*Suddenly and passionately, almost wildly.*] I ain't comin' down. You hear me? I ain't comin' down. [*He looks at* GABRIEL.] Go ahead, Gabriel. 'Tend to yo' chores. I'm gonter keep wukkin' yere.

GABRIEL

I hates to see you feelin' like dis, Lawd.

GOD

Dat's all right. Even bein' Gawd ain't a bed of roses. [GABRIEL *exits.* HOSEA's *shadow is on the wall. For a second* HOSEA *hesitates.* GOD *looks at the wall. Goes to window.*] I hear you. I know yo' fightin' bravely, but I ain't comin' down. Oh, why don' you leave me alone? You know you ain't talkin' to me. *Is* you talkin' to me? I cain't stand yo' talkin' dat way. I kin only hear part of what you' sayin', and it puzzles me. Don' you know you cain't puzzle God? [*A pause. Then tenderly.*] Do you want me to come down dere ve'y much? You know I said I wouldn't come down? [*Fiercely.*] Why don' he answer me a little? [*With clenched fists, looks down through the window.*] Listen! I'll tell you what I'll do. I ain't goin' to promise you anythin', and I ain't goin' to do nothin' to help you. I'm jest feelin' a little low, an' I'm only comin' down to make myself feel a little better, dat's all.

> [*The stage is darkened.* CHOIR *begins "A Blind Man Stood In De Middle of De Road," and continues until the lights go up on the next scene.*]

Scene VII

It is a shadowed corner beside the walls of the temple in Jerusalem. The light of camp fires flickers on the figure of HEZDREL, *who was* ADAM *in Part I. He stands in the same position* ADAM *held when first discovered but in his right hand is a sword, and his left is in a sling. Around him are several prostrate bodies. Pistol and cannon shots, then a trumpet call. Six young men enter from left in command of a* CORPORAL. *They are all armed.*

CORPORAL

De fightin's stopped fo' de night, Hezdrel.

HEZDREL

Yes?

CORPORAL

Dey're goin' to begin ag'in at cockcrow. [*Man enters, crosses the stage and exits.*] Herod say he's goin' to take de temple tomorrow, burn de books and de Ark of de Covenant, and put us all to de sword.

HEZDREL

Yo' ready, ain't you?

EVERYBODY

Yes, Hezdrel.

HEZDREL

Did de food get in through de hole in de city wall?
[*Two soldiers enter, cross the stage and exit.*]

CORPORAL

Yessuh, we's goin' back to pass it out now.

HEZDREL

Good. Any mo' of our people escape today?

CORPORAL

Ol' Herod's got de ol' hole covered up now, but fifteen of our people got out a new one we made.
[*Other soldiers enter, cross the stage and exit.*]

HEZDREL

Good. Take dese yere wounded men back and git 'em took care of.

CORPORAL

Yes, suh.
[*They pick up the bodies on the ground and carry them offstage as* HEZDREL *speaks.*]

HEZDREL

So dey gonter take de temple in de mo'nin'? We'll be waitin' for 'em. Jest remember, boys, when dey kill us we leap out of our skins, right into de lap of God.
[*The men disappear with the wounded; from the deep shadow upstage comes* GOD.]

GOD

Hello, Hezdrel—Adam.

HEZDREL

[*Rubbing his forehead.*] Who is you?

GOD

Me? I'm jest an ol' preacher, from back in de hills.

HEZDREL

What you doin' yere?

GOD

I heard you boys was fightin'. I jest wanted to see how it was goin'.

HEZDREL

Well, it ain't goin' so well.

GOD

Dey got you skeered, huh?

HEZDREL

Look yere, who is you, a spy in my brain?

GOD

Cain't you see I's one of yo' people?

HEZDREL

Listen, Preacher, we ain't skeered. We's gonter be killed, but we ain't skeered.

GOD

I's glad to hear dat. Kin I ask you a question, Hezdrel?

HEZDREL

What is it?

GOD

How is it you is so brave?

HEZDREL

Caize we got faith, dat's why!

GOD

Faith? In who?

HEZDREL

In our dear Lawd God.

GOD

But God say he abandoned ev' one down yere.

HEZDREL

Who say dat? Who dare say dat of de Lawd God of Hosea?

GOD

De God of Hosea?

HEZDREL

You heard me. Look yere, you *is* a spy in my brain!

[165]

GOD

No, I ain't, Hezdrel. I'm jest puzzled. You ought to know dat.

HEZDREL

How come you so puzzled 'bout de God of Hosea?

GOD

I don' know. Maybe I jest don' hear things. You see, I live 'way back in de hills.

HEZDREL

What you wanter find out?

GOD

Ain't de God of Hosea de same Jehovah dat was de God of Moses?

HEZDREL

[*Contemptuously.*] No. Dat ol' God of wrath and vengeance? We have de God dat Hosea preached to us. He's de one God.

GOD

Who's he?

HEZDREL

[*Reverently.*] De God of mercy.

GOD

Hezdrel, don' you think dey must be de same God?

[166]

HEZDREL

I don' know. I ain't bothered to think much about
it. Maybe dey is. Maybe our God is de same ol' God.
I guess we jest got tired of his appearance dat ol' way.

GOD

What you mean, Hezdrel?

HEZDREL

Oh, dat ol' God dat walked de earth in de shape of
a man. I guess he lived wid man so much dat all he
seen was de sins in man. Dat's what made him de God
of wrath and vengeance. Co'se he made Hosea. An'
Hosea never would a found what mercy was unless
dere was a little of it in God, too. Anyway, he ain't a
fearsome God no mo'. Hosea showed us dat.

GOD

How you s'pose Hosea found dat mercy?

HEZDREL

De only way he could find it. De only way I found
it. De only way anyone kin find it.

GOD

How's dat?

HEZDREL

Through sufferin'.

[167]

GOD

[*After a pause.*] What if dey kill you in de mo'nin' Hezdrel.

HEZDREL

If dey do, dey do. Dat's all.

GOD

Herod say he's goin' to burn de temple—

HEZDREL

So he say.

GOD

And burn de Ark an' de books. Den dat's de end of de books, ain't it?

HEZDREL

[*Buoyantly.*] What you mean? If he burns dem things in dere? Naw. Dem's jest copies.

GOD

Where is de others?

HEZDREL

[*Tapping his head.*] Dey's a set in yere. Fifteen got out through de hole in the city wall today. A hundred and fifty got out durin' de week. Each of em is a set of de books. Dey's scattered safe all over de countryside now, jest waitin' to git pen and paper fo' to put 'em down agin.

GOD

[*Proudly.*] Dey cain't lick you, kin dey Hezdrel?

HEZDREL

[*Smiling.*] I know dey cain't. [*Trumpet.*] You better get out o' yere, Preacher, if you wanter carry de news to yo' people. It'll soon be daylight.

GOD

I'm goin'. [*He takes a step upstage and stops.*] Want me to take any message?

HEZDREL

Tell de people in de hills dey ain't nobody like de Lawd God of Hosea.

GOD

I will. If dey kill you tomorrow I'll bet dat God of Hosea'll be waitin' for you.

HEZDREL

I *know* he will.

GOD

[*Quietly.*] Thank you, Hezdrel.

HEZDREL

Fo' what?

GOD

Fo' tellin' me so much. You see I been so far away, I guess I was jest way behin' de times.

[*He exits. Pause, then trumpet sounds.*]
[HEZDREL *paces back and forth once or twice. Another young soldier appears. Other men enter and stand grouped about* HEZDREL.]

SECOND OFFICER

[*Excitedly.*] De cock's jest crowed, Hezdrel. Dey started de fightin' ag'in.

HEZDREL

We's ready for 'em. Come on, boys. [*From the darkness upstage comes another group of soldiers.*] Dis is de day dey say dey'll git us. Le's fight till de last man goes. What d'you say?

CORPORAL

Le's go, Hezdrel!

HEZDREL

[*Calling left.*] Give 'em ev'ything, boys!
[*There is a movement toward the left, a bugle call and the sound of distant battle. The lights go out. The* CHOIR *is heard singing, "March On," triumphantly. They continue to sing after the lights go up on the next scene.*]

SCENE VIII

*It is the same setting as the Fish Fry Scene in Part I.
The same angels are present but the* CHOIR, *instead of
marching, is standing in a double row on an angle upstage right.* GOD *is seated in an armchair near center.
He faces the audience. As the* CHOIR *continues to sing,*
GABRIEL *enters, unnoticed by the chattering angels. He
looks at* GOD *who is staring thoughtfully toward the
audience.*

GABRIEL

You look a little pensive, Lawd. [GOD *nods his head.*]
Have a seegar, Lawd?

GOD

No thanks, Gabriel.
  [GABRIEL *goes to the table, accepts a cup of custard; chats with the angel behind the table for a
  moment as he sips, puts the cup down and returns to the side of* GOD.]

GABRIEL

You look awful pensive, Lawd. You been sittin' yere,
lookin' dis way, an awful long time. Is it somethin'
serious, Lawd?

GOD

Very serious, Gabriel.

[171]

GABRIEL

[*Awed by His tone.*] Lawd, is de time come for me
to blow?

GOD

Not yet, Gabriel. I'm just thinkin'.

GABRIEL

What about, Lawd? [*Puts up hand. Singing stops.*]

GOD

'Bout somethin' de boy tol' me. Somethin' 'bout
Hosea, and himself. How dey foun' somethin'.

GABRIEL

What, Lawd?

GOD

Mercy. [*A pause.*] Through *sufferin'*, he said.

GABRIEL

Yes, Lawd.

GOD

I'm tryin' to find it, too. It's awful impo'tant. It's
awful impo'tant to all de people on my earth. Did he
mean dat even God must suffer?

[GOD *continues to look out over the audience for a
moment and then a look of surprise comes into
his face. He sighs. In the distance a voice cries.*]

THE VOICE

Oh, look at him! Oh, look, dey goin' to make him carry it up dat high hill! Dey goin' to nail him to it! Oh, dat's a terrible burden for one man to carry!

[GOD *rises and murmurs "Yes!" as if in recognition. The heavenly beings have been watching him closely, and now, seeing him smile gently, draw back, relieved. All the angels burst into "Hallelujah, King Jesus." GOD continues to smile as the lights fade away. The singing becomes fortissimo.*

CURTAIN